Practical TensorFlow.js

Deep Learning in Web App Development

D0878843

Juan De Dios Santos Rivera

Apress®

Practical TensorFlow.js: Deep Learning in Web App Development

Juan De Dios Santos Rivera
San Juan, PR, USA

ISBN-13 (pbk): 978-1-4842-6272-6   ISBN-13 (electronic): 978-1-4842-6273-3
https://doi.org/10.1007/978-1-4842-6273-3

Managing Director, Apress Media LLC: Welmoed Spahr
Acquisitions Editor: Aaron Black
Development Editor: James Markham
Coordinating Editor: Jessica Vakili

Distributed to the book trade worldwide by Springer Science+Business Media New York, 1 NY Plaza, New York, NY 10014. Phone 1-800-SPRINGER, fax (201) 348-4505, e-mail orders-ny@springer-sbm.com, or visit www.springeronline.com. Apress Media, LLC is a California LLC and the sole member (owner) is Springer Science + Business Media Finance Inc (SSBM Finance Inc). SSBM Finance Inc is a **Delaware** corporation.

For information on translations, please e-mail booktranslations@springernature.com; for reprint, paperback, or audio rights, please e-mail bookpermissions@springernature.com.

Apress titles may be purchased in bulk for academic, corporate, or promotional use. eBook versions and licenses are also available for most titles. For more information, reference our Print and eBook Bulk Sales web page at http://www.apress.com/bulk-sales.

Any source code or other supplementary material referenced by the author in this book is available to readers on GitHub via the book's product page, located at www.apress.com/ 978-1-4842-6272-6. For more detailed information, please visit http://www.apress.com/ source-code.

Printed on acid-free paper

To friends and adventures.

Table of Contents

About the Author xiii

About the Technical Reviewers xv

Acknowledgments xvii

Introduction xix

Chapter 1: Welcome to TensorFlow.js 1

   Why the browser? 2

      JavaScript 2

      Accessibility 3

      Privacy 4

      Speed 4

      Cost-effectiveness 5

   Features 5

      Inference engine 5

      Pre-trained models 6

      Backend 7

      Compatibility with TensorFlow 8

   Architecture 10

      Tensors 10

      Layers API 12

      Operations API 15

   How to install 16

   Recap 18

Chapter 2: Training our first models 19

Approaching a machine learning problem 20

The data..20

The model..22

The training framework 23

Defining the model's architecture 23

The performance metric, loss function, and optimizer 23

Evaluating the model..25

Deploying the model..25

Building a logistic regression model...................................26

Understanding logistic regression.................................27

What is an artificial neural network? 29

Overview of the data 32

Building the app 33

Building a linear regression model 54

Understanding linear regression 54

Overview of the data 56

Building the app 57

Wrapping things up 75

Chapter 3: Doing k-means with ml5.js 77

Understanding k-means..78

About ml5.js 79

About the data...79

Building the app 79

Setting up the workspace and the app's HTML....................80

Training..83

Visualizing the clusters...85

Testing the model 87

Recap 89

Chapter 4: Recognizing handwritten digits with convolutional neural networks 91

Understanding convolutional neural networks 92

About the MNIST dataset 96

Building the app...97

The app's HTML file...98

Loading and preparing the data 99

Defining the network..105

Training the model..110

Creating the drawing canvas...114

Putting it all together...117

Trying the app...120

Recap and conclusion..122

Chapter 5: Making a game with PoseNet, a pose estimator model 125

What is PoseNet?..126

The COCO dataset 128

Building the game..129

Structuring the UI 129

Setting up the camera...133

Loading and testing the model...136

Creating the gameplay loop..141

Testing the game...148

Recap 148

Chapter 6: Identifying toxic text from a Google Chrome Extension 151

Understanding the toxicity detector 152

About the data 154

Building the extension 154

    Creating the HTML and app's manifest 155

    The extension script 157

    Deploying and testing the app 160

Recap 161

Chapter 7: Object detection with a model trained in Google Cloud AutoML 163

What is AutoML Vision Object Detection 165

About the model 166

About the data 166

Training the model 167

    Setting up your Google Cloud account 167

    Preparing the dataset 168

    Labeling and annotating the images 169

    Training 170

    Evaluate 170

    Exporting the model 172

Building the app 173

    Loading packages and preparing the UI 174

    Importing the model and setting up the camera 176

    Detecting the objects 178

    Drawing the bounding boxes 180

    Testing the app 181

Recap 183

Chapter 8: Training an image classifier with transfer learning on Node.js 185

What is transfer learning? 186

Understanding MobileNet and ImageNet 187

Building the Trainer 188

    Setting up the environment 188

    Loading and pre-processing the images 189

    Training the model with transfer learning 192

    Running the Trainer 195

Building the Server 197

    Serving the model 197

    Testing the model 200

Recap 200

Chapter 9: Time series forecasting and text generation with recurrent neural networks 203

Understanding RNN and LSTM 204

About the data 206

Building RNNs for time series forecasting 207

    Preparing the app's interface 207

    Transforming the dataset 210

    Designing the model and training it 214

    Predicting and testing the model 216

    Running the app 220

    Multiple timestep forecasting 221

Generating text using a pre-trained LSTM with ml5.js 232

    Developing the app 233

    Testing the app 236

Recap and conclusion 238

Chapter 10: Generating handwritten digits with generative adversarial networks 241

A friendly introduction to GANs...242

Training a GAN..244

    Preparing the environment...245

Getting the data 245

    Making the generator 250

    Making the discriminator 254

Combining the models 258

    Training the discriminator..261

    Training the combined model 263

    Putting it all together..264

Testing the app 266

Recap 269

Chapter 11: Things to remember, what's next for you, and final words..271

Things to remember...272

    Tensors 272

    Memory management 273

    TensorFlow.js Visualization (tfjs-vis).....................................274

    Designing a model..276

    Hyperparameters and attributes 277

    Testing 278

    Asynchronous code 279

What's next for you? 280

External resources 281

Thank you 282

Appendix A: Apache License 2.0...**283**

TERMS AND CONDITIONS FOR USE, REPRODUCTION, AND DISTRIBUTION 283

References...**291**

Index...**297**

About the Author

Juan De Dios Santos Rivera is a machine learning engineer who focuses on building data-driven and machine learning–driven platforms. As a Big Data Software Engineer, his role has been to build solutions to detect spammers and avoid their proliferation. This book goes hand in hand with that role in building data solutions. As the AI field keeps growing, developers need to keep extending the reach of our products to every platform out there, which includes web browsers. He holds a master of science degree in Computer Science from Uppsala University, Sweden.

About the Technical Reviewers

Mezgani Ali is a Ph.D. student in Artificial Intelligence (Mohammed V University in Rabat) and researcher at Native LABs, Inc. He likes technology, reading, and spending time with his daughter Ghita. His first program was a Horoscope in Basic in 1993. He has done a lot of work on the infrastructure side in system engineering and software engineering and managed networks and security.

Mezgani worked for NIC France, Capgemini, and HP and was part of the Site Reliability Engineer's (SRE) team that was responsible for keeping data center servers and customers' applications up and running. He is fanatical about Kubernetes, REST API, MySQL, and Scala and creator of the functional and imperative programming language PASP.

Massimo Nardone has more than 22 years of experience in security, web/mobile development, cloud, and IT architecture. His true IT passions are security and Android.

He has been programming and teaching how to program with Android, Perl, PHP, Java, VB, Python, C/C++, and MySQL for more than 20 years.

He holds a master of science degree in Computer Science from the University of Salerno, Italy.

He has worked as a Project Manager, Software Engineer, Research Engineer, Chief Security Architect, Information Security Manager, PCI/SCADA Auditor, and Senior Lead IT Security/Cloud/SCADA Architect for many years.

Acknowledgments

I wrote this book during my backpacking adventures through Asia and New Zealand. Before starting the trip, I told myself, "it would be amazing to write a book during this time." Luckily, and fortunately, on November 20, 2019, Aaron Black, Senior Editor from Apress, contacted me asking if I was interested in writing a book on TensorFlow.js. The answer was yes, and so I would like to first thank him for giving me such a fantastic opportunity. Also, from Apress, I want to thank Jessica Vakili, Coordinating Editor, for answering those little questions I had, and Technical Editors Ali Mezgani and Massimo Nardone for correcting my oversights.

To all my former LOVOO colleagues, thank you so much for all the help! Alexander Bresk, thanks for taking the time to review the introduction to artificial neural networks. Sergio Camilo Hernández, *gracias* for going through Chapter 1 and giving me that initial feedback, and Helton Luiz Marques for finding inconsistencies in Chapter 3.

To my friends: Jesús Luzón González, thanks for shedding some light on several definitions and for helping to correct Chapter 8. Jean Rodríguez Aulet for comments regarding the brain's visual cortex (Chapter 4). José Figueroa Salgado, Christos Sakalis, and Owen Baxter for making sure the introduction catches the reader. Daniel Llatas Spiers for correcting several concepts. To Nancy Wächtler, *vielen dank* for helping with the designs of the figures. To Vincent Warmerdam, thanks for taking the time to go over the USE explanation from Chapter 6. Felipe Hoffa, thanks for taking a look at the introduction to the Google Cloud section from Chapter 7.

Introduction

Many celebrated works of science fiction portray a futuristic Earth as a planet occupied by flying cars, otherworldly structures, and artificial intelligence. The latter is, to some extent, now a reality. But this type of artificial intelligence (AI) is different from what we see in the movies. There are no sentient or organic robots, know-it-all virtual assistants, or computers with a human conscience. Instead, the AI we are currently experiencing focuses on a subtle component of intelligence: prediction. In their book *Prediction Machines*, the economists Ajay Agrawal, Avi Goldfarb, and Joshua Gans define prediction as "the process of filling in missing information" using as a basis previous information, better known as **data**.

Data is the backbone of a predictive system. The more you have, the better the system learns. Nowadays, thanks to the advances in computing power, cheaper storage, accessible Internet, the interconnectivity between us, and the advent of the modern mobile device, we are amassing data on an unprecedented scale. But by itself, data does not do much. It needs a model to consume it and learn from it.

The discipline of artificial intelligence that involves predictive systems is called **machine learning**. This discipline studies algorithms that use data to learn a task without being explicitly programmed. For example, a machine learning model that sees many pictures of cats will eventually learn to identify cats.

While AI is not a new concept, after their first groundbreaking discoveries in the 1950s and 1960s, the public interest, funding, and development of AI projects decreased significantly. This period is known as the "AI Winter" in the community. In the late 2000s, the field of artificial intelligence awoke from its slumber. This resurfacing is often attributed to the publication of two computer vision papers by Geoffrey Hinton and Alex Krizhevsky. Hinton developed a neural network capable of recognizing handwritten digits, while Krizhevsky created a neural network architecture capable of classifying everyday objects with state-of-the-art accuracy. These papers coined the name "deep learning," a term used to refer to deep artificial neural networks.

The achievements of these two deep networks put machine learning back in the spotlight and started a wave of innovation and interest that has no foreseeable end. In the last ten years, machine learning and deep learning models have been applied to a range of use cases, such as image classification, object detection, forecasting, text and image generation, speech recognition, and language translation. More impressive is that some of these models outperform humans at the same task. So now that we have the theory to understand these networks, the data to feed them, the computing power to handle them, and the interest of the industry and academic communities to try deep learning, what we need is more frameworks to train them in your platform of choice. This last reason brings us to TensorFlow.js and this book.

About the book

TensorFlow.js is a machine learning framework for developing and serving artificial neural network–based models in **JavaScript**, the language of the Web, directly on your web browser. In this book, *Practical TensorFlow.js*, you will learn and explore, through hands-on examples, how to develop and deploy models using TensorFlow.js.

As the title states, in this book, we will focus on practical use cases, applications that go further than just training models. For example, in one chapter, you will build a game, and in another, a Google Chrome Extension. The apps you will write here do not end at the browser. In the later chapters, you will learn how to run TensorFlow.js server-side using Node.js to train and deploy a model. Since we are in a web environment, building web applications, the examples include basic web development concepts. But do not worry if you do not have a web development background because the book also explains those parts.

Some machine learning applications we will cover in the book include image classification, object detection, natural language processing, transfer learning, and time series analysis. You will explore them using networks such as convolutional neural networks, recurrent neural networks, and generative adversarial networks and "traditional" machine learning algorithms like linear regression. However, you will not implement all of them. One feature of TensorFlow.js is the availability of several pre-trained models for various scenarios. Through our adventures, we will learn how to use some of them.

While the book focuses on the practical side of deep learning, before each exercise, there is a brief review of the model involved in the chapter. Last, to extend the reach of the examples, you will use other tools and frameworks like TensorFlow.js Visualization, Google Cloud, TensorBoard, and ml5.js.

Who is this book for?

This book targets those interested in developing deep learning solutions for the Web with TensorFlow.js. You do not need previous machine learning experience. However, it would help at least knowing what it is. For the beginner out there, firstmost, welcome to the exciting field of machine learning! This book will give you the right tools and knowledge to get you started in your machine learning (ML) path. After finishing it, you will be able to understand neural networks, a variety of them, and their uses. Most importantly, after the book, you will be capable of developing neural networks using TensorFlow.js, building applications around the networks, and deploying them on different platforms.

To the expert, the chances are that you come from a Python background. If so, with this book, you will learn how to develop your models using TensorFlow.js Keras-like API or train them in Google Cloud, how to bring existing models to TensorFlow.js, and how to serve them in Node.js.

The book assumes that you have experience programming and doing software development since we will be writing code hands-on and using technical terms like "server," "Git," and "backend." The book's main language is JavaScript, so it would help to know the basics of it. Nonetheless, the book assumes that you do not know it, and so it explains those details that might be confusing or particular to the language. The goal here is that you will fully understand every detail behind the exercises.

Structure

Most of the chapters in the book consist of five principal sections. These are an introduction, an overview of the model, an explanation of the dataset, the application, and a recap.

Introduction

In the introduction, I will present the problem we will solve, the model or algorithm used to solve the problem, and the frameworks or libraries we will see throughout the chapter.

The model

In this part, we will learn about the model, its characteristics, peculiarities, and how it works.

The dataset

This brief section describes the dataset we will use to train the model.

The application

Here, we will build the application. Since most of the exercises are web apps, we will start by designing its interface in an HTML file. Then, we will proceed to build the functionalities.

Recap and further exercises

To end each chapter, we will see a small recap of the main terms and lessons discovered, followed by further exercises you could do to keep building on what you learned.

The source code

You will write the exercises in JavaScript and use HTML and CSS for the interface and styling. The JavaScript code follows the ESLint coding style. During the explanations, I will (usually) present the code snippets split by functions, for example:

```
function foo() {
}
```

And in another code snippet:

```
function bar() {
}
```

However, on some occasions, when the function is long, I will divide it across several code chunks. In those cases, I will explicitly indicate that the following code goes after the previous line.

All of the exercises' code is available on GitHub at `https://github.com/Apress/Practical-TensorFlow.js`. There, you will find a directory per chapter with the complete code and datasets.

Now, without further ado, let me welcome you to TensorFlow.js. I hope you will enjoy this adventure. Follow me!

CHAPTER 1

Welcome to TensorFlow.js

The world is on the verge of an **artificial intelligence** (AI) revolution. This wave of innovation, which takes the shape of **data** and **machine learning** (ML), is rapidly changing the way we create software, how industries function, and even facets of our lives. As the adoption and demand for data-based products and machine learning–powered applications increase, so do their requirements, the tools used to develop them, and the platforms where we wish to deploy them. One of these platforms is the **web browser**.

Although accessible, for a long time, the browser was not regarded as a potential medium capable of harnessing and serving the power of **machine learning**. However, as the field keeps evolving and we march toward an Age of Data, the browser is slowly proving itself as a worthy contender, one that can deliver the breakthroughs of machine learning because of the advantages and distinctive features it possesses.

Born from the necessity to have a reliable and production-ready solution for doing machine learning on the Web, the TensorFlow team released **TensorFlow.js** in March 2018. This library is a high-performance and open source framework for training, executing, and deploying ML models in the browser using **JavaScript** (JS).

© Juan De Dios Santos Rivera 2020
J. Rivera, *Practical TensorFlow.js*, https://doi.org/10.1007/978-1-4842-6273-3_1

TensorFlow.js is the successor of *deeplearn.js*, a defunct machine learning tool developed by Google Brain for building artificial neural network–based models for the browser. Now, this library is at the center of TensorFlow.js and bears the name **TensorFlow.js Core API** or just **tfjs-core**.

According to the paper "TensorFlow.js: Machine Learning for the Web and Beyond" (Smilkov et al., 2019), one of the main motivations behind TF.js is bringing to JavaScript and the web ecosystem the power of machine learning to JS developers and to those with limited or no ML experience. TF.js achieves this goal thanks to its multiple abstraction levels, which provide an easy-to-use and clean experience without compromising the functionality.

Why the browser?

Doing and executing machine learning have been mainly associated with *Python, R, C++*, servers, cloud, GPU, and CPU—but not the browser. Or at least until the first machine learning libraries surfaced. But why now? What is making the web browser a desirable platform for executing ML? We could argue and agree that these are some valid reasons: JavaScript, accessibility, privacy, speed, and cost-effectiveness.

JavaScript

As stated in GitHub's 2019 report titled "The State of the Octoverse" (GitHub, 2019) and StackOverflow's Developer Survey (StackOverflow, 2019), JavaScript is (and has been for at least seven years) the world's most popular programming language. It beat Python, one that has been in the spotlight for a few years now because of its status as the de facto language of "data science." Being the top language implies that it has both demand and supply—the demand for more products and the developers to supply them. Yet, for a long time, until 2015, when libraries such as *ConvNetJS*, *brain.js*, and eventually TensorFlow.js were released, there was no competitive or production-ready framework to develop and execute deep learning on the browser. So, given the popularity of the language, it was only a matter of time before the deep learning revolution reached this large group of developers.

Moreover, JavaScript is slowly turning into a language capable of doing production-ready machine learning and data science. In recent years, JavaScript has gained other libraries and frameworks such as *Apache Arrow*,[1] a language-agnostic framework for processing columnar data, *Observable*[2] (notebook), and many visualization tools that assist us at evaluating data.

Accessibility

When you are on your computer or mobile device, what's the app you are most likely to use? …Exactly! The web browser, our gateway to the Web, and a very accessible tool. Now consider all the people who use a browser and multiply that by the time spent clicking and getting lost amid the entanglement of the World Wide Web. That has to be a considerable number. With such a broad audience, it would seem like the web browser is an ideal place to deploy machine learning applications.

But not only is the web browser a medium accessible to most of us. The nature of the browser itself has access to a wide range of components, such as the device's microphone, web camera, keyboard, location, and many sensors (like an accelerometer) if the computer supports them. These tools are sources of data—handy and rich data that can power many ML models.

---

[1]https://arrow.apache.org/docs/js
[2]https://observablehq.com

Privacy

As great and powerful as the aforementioned data is, some of us would be reluctant to give it away in exchange, for example, of a service that could predict if you look tired today based on an image. But with TensorFlow.js and its **on-device** installed models, the user does not have to worry about this. With a model deployed on the browser—and not on an external server where you would have to send your data somewhere else—the provided data and the model's predictions stay on your device.

This preservation of the user's privacy enables developers to create applications that use sensitive data, for instance, services for the medical industry and silly ones like the "tired or not" app mentioned earlier. In such a case, you will be able to use the app, knowing that nobody would ever see your sleepy morning face.

Speed

Another advantage of having an on-device model doing its computations client-side is the gain in speed. Hosting the model client-side means not having to upload data somewhere else, allowing us to reduce the overall latency of the application and the inference time. This advantage is beneficial when the application involves large datasets such as imagery or audio data. For example, suppose that our "tired or not" app has an even better predictive model that uses a 5-second clip instead of an image. Now imagine having to upload that video, waiting for the computation, and downloading the result. That is at least a few seconds. Sure, a few seconds is nothing, but in other kinds of applications, for example, real-time object detection, this latency would undoubtedly be detrimental.

Cost-effectiveness

Suppose that we present our "tired or not" web app at the *Tired People World Convention*, and it wins the "Best of Show" award. Wow, congrats! As a result, the app suddenly goes viral, and millions of users are checking if they are tired. In an unfortunate pre-TensorFlow.js scenario where we would host the model somewhere in the cloud, we would have to pay for the bandwidth involved in the traffic. Besides, the service is most likely to crash since we went from two users to millions in less than an hour. As a result, now we need to scale up and start a couple of additional machines, and this is not cheap at all.

However, since we know TensorFlow.js, and how to deploy models on the browser, the total cost might be a fraction of that paid in the earlier example. Still, the app has to download the model, but as we will later see, they can be as small as less than 1 MB.

Features

As we will discover in the book and its exercise, TensorFlow.js is an extensive and complete ecosystem with a multitude of functionalities. Of these, there are four that distinguish it and make it a unique library among the deep learning frameworks currently available. These features are its usage as an **inference engine**, the **pre-trained models**, its many **backends**, and the **compatibility with TensorFlow**.

Inference engine

While TensorFlow.js is a complete deep learning framework that supports building machine learning models, it truly excels as an inference engine, a tool for performing predictions. The opposite of a prediction engine is a solution specialized for training models, for example, *TensorFlow* or *PyTorch*.[3] Typically, after training a model, if we wish to deploy it to production, we must consider alternative platforms such as a custom API service, a cloud solution like *Google's AI Platform*,[4] *TensorFlow Lite* (an inference engine for mobile devices), and of course, TensorFlow.js. With the former, we can quickly train, deploy, and present the model to a user directly in the browser, making it an ideal inference engine.

Pre-trained models

A second feature that relates to the previous one is how simple it is to load pre-trained models that work out of the box. TensorFlow.js comes with several built-in models that cover a whole range of use cases. For example, if you need a quick object detector to make sure the person using the "tired or not" app is, well, a person, TF.js provides a model trained on the COCO dataset. To load it and use it, we only need two lines of code, such as this:

```
// Load the model.
const model = await cocoSsd.load();

// Classify the image.
const predictions = await model.detect(img);
```

Likewise, if you are ever in need of a classifier that detects whether a piece of text contains toxic content (insults, threats, obscenity), there is a text toxicity detection model available in TF.js (one exercise from the book features this model). Table 1-1 presents some models provided by TensorFlow.js and ml5.js, a high-level library built on top of TensorFlow.js that we will use later in the book.

---

[3]https://pytorch.org
[4]https://cloud.google.com/ai-platform

Table 1-1. *Some pre-trained models*

Use Case	Description
Body segmentation	Segments a person's body part with BodyPix
Object detection	SSD model trained with the COCO dataset
Sentence encoding	Encodes text into embeddings
k-means (ml5.js)	Clusters data using k-means

Backend

A highlight of TensorFlow.js is that it supports three unique backends that also dictate how it runs under the hood. These backends are **WebGL**, **Node.js**, and **regular** JavaScript. Each of these solutions has its own set of advantages and disadvantages that are mostly perceived in the speed of the operations.

WebGL

Training a large neural network is a computationally intensive task. On top of that, inferring a result can also, in the worst-case scenario, take a few seconds. To deal with these drawbacks, developers resort to big and expensive machines equipped with powerful and expensive graphics processing units (GPUs) to train these models. What distinguishes a GPU is its ability to do many numerical computations in parallel, something that a CPU can do, but not as effective as it.

One of the TensorFlow.js backend modes is the **WebGL** mode, one that uses your computer's GPU to accelerate and parallelize its processes. WebGL is a JavaScript API for rendering high-performance interactive graphics in the browser. While the original purpose of this library is to render those flashy graphics we see online nowadays, the developers behind TensorFlow.js are using it to improve and speed up its processes and performance. The WebGL mode is the default one, as long as your browser supports it.

Node.js

Another backend is the "node" mode that enables running TensorFlow. js in a Node.js application. Node.js is a JavaScript server-side runtime that executes JS code in an environment outside the browser. Running TF.js in Node.js has many advantages, with the biggest one being the capability of performing server-side, allowing us to build applications that do not have to interact with the user directly. An example would be deploying a different version of *tired or not* in a server and exposing it with a web service.

A second advantage of using a Node.js backend is the gain in performance. For instance, in a Node.js environment, TensorFlow.js uses the TensorFlow C library, which is faster than the JS implementation. Moreover, the Node.js backend features a GPU variant that accelerates tensor operations by running them on an NVIDIA GPU using CUDA.

Regular CPU

Then, there is the least performant CPU backend, which uses a plain JS implementation of TensorFlow.js. Its advantage is that the package size is the smallest of all of them. This mode is the fallback option.

Compatibility with TensorFlow

As the name points out, TensorFlow.js is part of the TensorFlow ecosystem. As a result, its Layers API and the overall way to develop a model resemble TensorFlow's Keras high-level API. Thanks to this consistency, transitioning from TF to TF.js (or the other way around) should be smoother for users familiar with one of the platforms. In the following code, you will find two examples of the same model in both TensorFlow.js and Keras.

TensorFlow.js:

```
const model = tf.sequential();

model.add(tf.layers.dense({
  inputShape: 1,
  units: 1,
  activation: 'sigmoid',
}));

model.compile({
  optimizer: tf.train.adam(0.1),
  loss: 'binaryCrossentropy',
  metrics: ['accuracy'],
});
```

TensorFlow 2.0 Keras Sequential model (Python):

```
model = tf.keras.Sequential()

model.add(tf.keras.layers.Dense(units=1,
          input_shape=[1]))

model.compile(optimizer='adam',
              loss='binary_crossentropy',
              metrics=['accuracy'])
```

But more than merely having a similar API, being a part of the TensorFlow ecosystem means being able to convert models originally trained in TensorFlow and even models from *TensorFlow Hub*[5]—a repository of TensorFlow's models—to TensorFlow.js models using a Python library named *TensorFlow.js Converter*.[6] During this conversion process, the library ensures that each operation from the original graph is compatible with those available in TensorFlow.js. Moreover, the tool provides various mechanisms that help to reduce the size of the model, which is always great when working in a web environment. Nonetheless, this process might compromise the model's predictive power, so be cautious.

Architecture

The TensorFlow.js library comprises two APIs: the **Operations API** and the **Layers API**. The former, Operations API, provides the essential low-level functionalities the library requires, like the mathematical and tensor operations, while the latter provides the basic blocks needed to build the models. But before getting there, to understand the next parts better and to give some context to the name "TensorFlow," let's see what a tensor is.

Tensors

Tensors are the main abstraction and unit of data of TensorFlow.js. More precisely, we could describe them as a multidimensional array or as the official documentation says, "a set of values shaped into an array of one and more dimensions" (Google, 2018b). In TF.js, tensors are objects, and

---

[5]https://tfhub.dev
[6]https://github.com/tensorflow/tfjs/tree/master/tfjs-converter

they have the following properties that describe them: **dtype, rank**, and **shape**. The first one, dtype, defines the tensor's data type; the second one, rank, describes how many dimensions the tensor has; and the last, shape, specifies the size of the dimensions of the data.

For example, the following code

```
const a = tf.tensor([[1, 2], [3, 4]]);
console.log(`${a.dtype} | ${a.shape} | ${a.rank}`);
```

outputs float32 | 2,2 | 2, which corresponds to a tensor whose elements are floats, shape is 2,2 (like a matrix), and rank is 2.

To have a proper idea of how something so abstract like a tensor looks like, Figure 1-1 presents five tensors of rank 1 up to rank 5. In the image, we can see that a tensor of rank 1 is a vector or an array. A tensor of rank 2 is a matrix, and a tensor of rank 3 is a cube. Then it gets more complex. A rank 4 tensor is a vector of cubes, and one of rank 5 is a matrix of cubes. As a concrete example, consider a colored image. When converted to a tensor, a colored image is represented with a tensor of rank 3, while a list of images is represented with a tensor of rank 4.

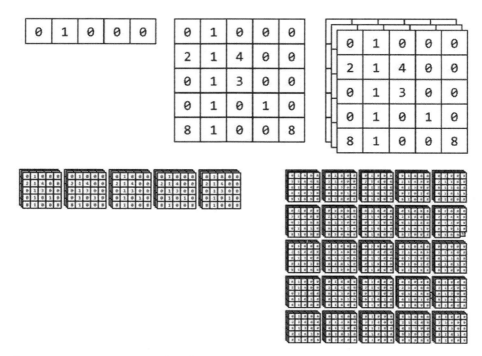

Figure 1-1. *An example of a tensor of ranks 1, 2, 3, 4, and 5*

But what about the "flow" part? The word "flow" refers to how the tensors move through the layers. As we will see later, when we define our first models, you will get the impression that defining the model is specifying how the data, or tensors, flow through the layers of the neural network. Besides this, not only tensors flow, but they also change their shapes and ranks, adding more sense to the "flow" term.

Layers API

The Layers API is TensorFlow.js' principal and preferred way of building the models we will train. It is a high-level API that works with the notion of stacking or connecting the layers in which the data will flow. If you have used Keras before, you will realize how similar it is to this library; as stated earlier, TF.js aims to be consistent with its counterpart TensorFlow.

The Layers API features two ways to make a model. The first, and most popular one, named **Sequential**, builds models by sequentially stacking layers so that the output of one is the input of the following one. Think of a stack of delicious fluffy pancakes where you add a ridiculously amount of syrup on the top, and as a result, the syrup will propagate or *flow* to the next layer. Let's illustrate with code how we can define a small neural network of two layers:

```
const model = tf.sequential();
model.add(tf.layers.dense({ inputShape: [10],
  activation: 'sigmoid', units: 10 }));
model.add(tf.layers.dense({ activation: 'softmax',
  units: 3 }));
```

To define a Sequential model, start by creating an instance of a tf.Sequential object, here named model. Then, with the method tf.Sequential.add(), we append the layers. The first of them is a dense layer with inputShape—the shape of the layer's input data—of 10. Following it is the units value—the layer's output shape—of also 10. Right after this layer, we add a second dense layer whose input shape is 10 and the output 3. Note that the input shape has to match the output of the previous one. Otherwise, the model won't compile. Figure 1-2 is a visual representation of the model's architecture and the dense layers. On the left-hand side of the first layer are the model's inputs, formally known as the input layer, followed by the "internal" units, or the hidden layer. The second layer receives as input the output of the previous layer and produces an output. This output part is called the output layer.

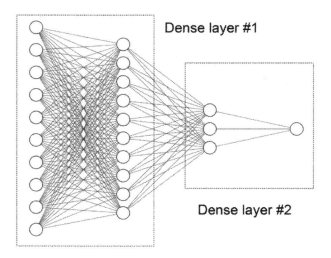

Figure 1-2. *Illustration of a model with two dense layers. Image was created using the software NN-SVG (LeNail, 2019)*

The second way of constructing models with the Layers API is using the **Functional** approach. The main difference is that, unlike the sequential method, this one allows creating the network's graph arbitrarily, as long as there are no cycles. Also, there is no add() method, but one called tf.layers.Layer.apply() that connects the layer. In the following, you will find the same model as before defined using the functional way:

```
const input = tf.input({ shape: [10] });
const dense1 = tf.layers.dense({ units: 10,
  activation: 'sigmoid' }).apply(input);
const dense2 = tf.layers.dense({ units: 3,
  activation: 'softmax'}).apply(dense1);
const model = tf.model({ inputs: input, outputs:
  dense2 });
```

The apply function returns an instance of an object known as a *SymbolicTensor*, which is a type of tensor that has no concrete value. Think of it as a placeholder for a tensor. The equivalent of this approach in a pancake world is having the pancakes laid down on a table and connecting them with lines of syrup (good luck cleaning that).

The Layers API goes beyond connecting layers. It includes a vast collection of tools such as `tf.Sequential.summary()`, a function that prints the model's structure and is helpful if you ever need to inspect it. In the exercises, we will get to know this method and others.

Operations API

The second API component is the Operations API. This one includes the low-level mathematical operations that we inadvertently apply each time we execute an action that involves a layer. These operations cover a whole range of mathematical scenarios, such as arithmetical operations that add two tensors element-wise, like this:

```
tf.tensor1d([1, 2]).add(tf.tensor1d([3,4])).print();
```

It also supports basic math operations like `tf.abs()` (absolute value), matrix operations, normalization methods, and logical operations. Because tensors are immutable objects, all operations return new tensors.

While using the Layers API is the standard and even the recommended (Google, 2018a) way of building a model, we should know that it is possible to create a model using the Operations API. Building a model using this approach provides us with full control of every part of the system. Despite this advantage, with this method, we would have to implement manually many of the features that the Layers API does for us, for example, training monitoring and weight initialization.

The following code presents the same model we have been using in this section implemented with operations:

```
function opModel() {
  const w1 = tf.variable(tf.randomNormal([10, 10]));
  const b1 = tf.variable(tf.randomNormal([10]));
  const w2 = tf.variable(tf.randomNormal([10, 3]));
  const b2 = tf.variable(tf.randomNormal([3]));

  // where x is a tensor of shape [10, 10]
  const model = (x) =>
    x.matMul(w1).add(b1).sigmoid().matMul(w2)
    .add(b2)
    .softmax();
}
```

How to install

After so much talk about TensorFlow.js, you might be very excited to implement the world's next big app. But before getting there and lifting another "Best of Show" award, we need to install the library. So, how do we do this? The first detail we need to decide is where we will execute our apps. Is it on the browser? Or as a Node.js application?

If it is for the browser (this is the most common case and the one we will use in this book), then there are two alternatives. The first one involves loading TensorFlow.js via a *content delivery network* (CDN) using a script tag. To access it this way, add the following tag to the app's main HTML file:

```
<script
 src="https://cdn.jsdelivr.net/npm/@tensorflow/tfjs">
</script>
```

Upon executing the app, this small line downloads and loads the library, saving us from manually installing it in our computers.

An alternate approach involves using a package manager like *npm* or *yarn* to download TensorFlow.js and add it to the project. In the following, you will find the commands

```
yarn add @tensorflow/tfjs
```

or

```
npm install @tensorflow/tfjs
```

Once the project is set, importing the library requires adding the following line to the JS script:

```
import * as tf from '@tensorflow/tfjs';
```

or

```
const tf = require('@tensorflow/tfjs');
```

If the target platform is Node.js, then use

```
yarn add @tensorflow/tfjs-node
```

or

```
npm install @tensorflow/tfjs-node
```

To install the GPU variant, use

```
yarn add @tensorflow/tfjs-node-gpu
```

or

```
npm install @tensorflow/tfjs-node-gpu
```

Recap

The applications and reach of machine learning are taking the world by storm. In its wake, this AI revolution is bringing a surge of smart products that are slowly shaping the way we lead our digital lives and even starting to disrupt the "real world." We have felt its effects. For instance, ML is improving the way we shop (not improving our wallets, though), how we browse movies, and even how we find love by matching us with the "perfect" target. Moreover, ML has also reached diverse platforms such as **mobile**, for example, *Google Assistant*, *Siri*, and *Android's Adaptive Battery*, and **embedded devices**, for example, *NVIDIA Jetson*. However, a platform that hasn't yet been impacted as the others is the web browser. Or so it was until TensorFlow.js came around.

TensorFlow.js is a deep learning library that aims to bring the AI revolution to JavaScript and the web browser. It provides the tools needed to create and deploy client-side low-latency models that require no server.

With over 12K stars on GitHub, TensorFlow.js is currently the most popular machine learning library for JavaScript. Granted that, we have to recognize the libraries that came before it and the others who are still active. Before TensorFlow.js, there was deeplearn.js, a package that now forms the core of TF.js. Other past libraries are *ConvNetJS* and *Keras.js*, and some that are still active are *brain.js* (10.6K stars) and ml5.js (3.4K stars).

So, what's next? In the next chapter, we will explore the basic building blocks of TensorFlow.js and use them to build our first models. Are you ready?

CHAPTER 2

Training our first models

In Chapter 1, we introduced the TensorFlow.js ecosystem. There, we discussed its history, features, and details, such as tensors, operations, and layers. In this second chapter, we will apply several of the concepts introduced to build our first machine learning models.

The models we will create here belong to the category of **supervised learning**. This is the ML task of learning from a labeled training set, a function that maps a set of inputs, known as **features**, to a **label** (also named class). In this chapter, we will explore this type of learning and how it works by building a **logistic regression** and **linear regression** model using TensorFlow.js' Layers API.

The first of these models, logistic regression, is a classic supervised learning model that classifies an instance into one of two classes. Then, we will see linear regression, an algorithm used to predict a numeric value. In Chapter 3, we will put supervised learning aside and focus on unsupervised learning, a type of machine learning that requires no labels.

Before heading straight to the algorithms, let's dedicate the first portion of the chapter to discuss how we will approach the machine learning projects you will build here (and in the rest of the book).

© Juan De Dios Santos Rivera 2020
J. Rivera, *Practical TensorFlow.js*, https://doi.org/10.1007/978-1-4842-6273-3_2

Approaching a machine learning problem

The starting point of every machine learning problem is precisely that: *the problem*, the thing we need to solve. This problem should not be building a machine learning model. Building a model is the solution or the approach we take to solve the problem. Instead, this problem should be a precise statement or question that, at the same time, could be translated into the objective we wish our model to learn.

Knowing what we want to solve is essential. Once we define the problem, we will be better positioned to select an adequate **model** (and thus, the learning paradigm) and other things that come with developing an ML system, for instance, the **training framework**, **performance metric**, and **deployment platform**. But, before that, there is one crucial detail we need to address, and that is the **data**—the fuel of machine learning.

The data

In machine learning, data is the essence. It is the information and knowledge that models use to learn. Without it, machine learning wouldn't exist. Oxford defines data as "facts and statistics collected together for reference or analysis."[1] I want to emphasize the word "analysis." In layman's terms, we could say that when a machine learning model is learning, it is analyzing the data until it is capable of extrapolating from it.

But, when we do machine learning, computers aren't the only ones that should analyze this data and learn from it. We, the humans responsible for the ML system, should analyze it too before feeding it to the model because of two main reasons.

---

[1]`www.lexico.com/en/definition/data`

The first of these is to assure the quality of the data. Bad and unclean data exists. In fact, I'm willing to say that most datasets are very far from being perfect. Therefore, we should dedicate a part of our development process to explore this data, pre-process it, and make sure it is suitable for our problem. After all, like we like to say in this field, "garbage in, garbage out," meaning that if the training data is poor, so is the model's predictive power.

The task of exploring a dataset is nonsurprisingly known as **exploratory data analysis**, and it involves summarizing, visualizing, and processing the data to learn more about it. While doing so, we may perform tasks such as *feature normalizing*, which is converting the numerical values to a common scale or checking for rows with empty values. Most of the datasets we will see in this book are already prepared and do not need any further modification. Still, it is always good to keep this in mind.

The second reason why it is essential to understand the data is that no model is compatible with every piece of data. Data comes in different sizes and shapes and has specific attributes, and unfortunately, there is no universal model that fits all. Of all the possible characteristics a dataset can have, the ones we will consider are the **type** of data and the **target variable**.

Some of the most used and popular types of data are **tabular**, **imagery**, and **text** data. A tabular dataset is the classic matrix. Its data is structured into rows and columns, where each row represents one particular instance or data observation, and the columns represent the properties or features—we typically find them in a *CSV* file. Then, there's imagery data, a format that is highly popular in deep learning. As we saw in Chapter 1, when we discussed tensors, images and videos are an extension of a tabular dataset. For example, a picture, at least a grayscale one, is a matrix where each data point is the intensity of a pixel. Last, there is also text data. This kind of data has no particular format. For instance, you can find text data in a tabular dataset, for example, a CSV file where each row is a sentence or in a corpus (large body of text). Text data is mostly used in natural language processing applications (NLP).

21

Then there are the target variables and its two kinds: **discrete** and **continuous**. A discrete variable is a variable that takes a specific value from a set of possible values. For instance, in a model whose goal is predicting whether this image is of a cat or a dog, the target variable is discrete because the only possible values are "cat" or "dog."

On the other hand, we have the continuous variables, which can take as a value any number between a minimum and a maximum value. Its target variable (what we want to predict) could be, for example, the distance I would walk in one day. In a case like this, the range of this variable goes from 0 km all the way to infinite (I better get some good shoes!).

The model

There is not a perfect machine learning model. While impressive, all of them have their advantages and disadvantages. Some do better on dataset *A* and not on *B*, while others perform great on *B* and not *A*—a concept known as *the no free lunch* theorem. So, choosing an appropriate one is not a trivial task. As mentioned in the previous point, the model is closely related to the kind of data we have at hand. For instance, images, due to their visual nature and large size, require a type of layer capable of extracting their features. So, for this case, a *convolutional neural network* (CNN) is a good choice. But for text data, CNN is not optimal. Instead, you could consider using *recurrent neural networks* (RNNs). Other cases include using *linear regression* if the goal is predicting a continuous value or logistic regression for discrete classification.

Selecting the model also depends on whether or not the dataset has labels. For example, in cases where the data is labeled, then the answer is a supervised learning model. Otherwise, unsupervised learning might be more appropriate.

Most of the models we will apply in this book belong to the **connectionism** field (Domingos, 2015), the one that involves artificial neural networks. Some will be deep networks, others shallow, and a few might not have the term "network" on their name, but they are still networks. Also, we will mostly focus on supervised learning problems.

The training framework

After getting the correct data and choosing the model, the following step is selecting the framework or library for training the model. In most cases, this is a personal choice or one based on the technology stack where we have to deploy the system. Some of the most popular ones are **TensorFlow** (Python), **PyTorch** (Python), **scikit-learn** (Python, see the trend?), and of course, **TensorFlow.js** (JavaScript).

Defining the model's architecture

In most libraries that do what some call "traditional machine learning"— ML that is not deep learning—training a model is a matter of creating an instance of the algorithm and using `model.fit()` to train it. In TensorFlow. js, this approach is not possible. As we saw in Chapter 1, defining a model in TensorFlow.js involves creating it layer by layer using the Layers API. For our exercises, we will use a mix of models we will design and train, pre-trained models, and ml5.js models.

The performance metric, loss function, and optimizer

Another part of the training we need to configure is the *performance metric*, a single number score that evaluates the correctness of the model. Once again, there is no perfect performance metric, and like the previous cases, it also depends on the data and the problem we are trying to solve.

Of all the performance metrics out there, the **accuracy** score is the most common one. This score measures the fraction or ratio of predictions the model correctly guessed. For example, suppose we have trained a model that predicts if a potato tastes good or not. Then, we test it with a test dataset of ten observations from which we know the ground truth (the real label). From these ten trials, seven of them were correct and three were not, so we could simplify this as saying that the model is 7 / 10 = 0.7 or 70% accurate (and that you just ate ten potatoes).

While straightforward and easy to interpret, the accuracy metric is not optimal for every case, for example, in problems where the target variable is continuous or situations where the dataset is imbalanced—when the number of observations of a class heavily outweighs another one, for instance, a dataset where 95% of the rows belong to class A.

A second aspect of the training we need to define is the *loss function*, often called the *cost* or *objective* function. This function specifies the objective the model wants to minimize during training. Like the performance metric, it is also a single number value. But instead of measuring its performance, it computes how incorrect the predictions are. During training, we want to minimize this value (we are not interested in wrong predictions, right?), so the smallest the number, the better it is.

There is no unique way to compute the loss value; after all, there are many loss functions. But the common ground between them is that the model evaluates it at the end of every batch of data and epoch (more on this soon). Then, it updates its weights (the model's parameters) according to the function's value: the loss value. It might be a bit tricky to grasp this concept, but after training the first model, you will get a better idea.

Last, we have a third component, the *optimizer*, another type of function that works very closely with the loss. In the preceding point, we said that the loss function intends to measure how wrong the model is so that it can update the weights. But by how much will it update those weights? That's the role of the optimizer. Quoting the official TensorFlow.js documentation, an optimizer's job is to "decide how much to change each parameter in the model given the current model prediction" (Google, 2018c).

Now, with the right data at hand, the model architecture defined, and the metrics decided, it's time to train our model.

Evaluating the model

Training a model can be a lengthy, expensive, and energy-hungry process. Hence, we need to make sure it proceeds in the right way to avoid any unpleasant surprises once the training ends. In the examples we are about to see, we will use the metrics introduced earlier to peek at the training and watch its progress. To do so, we will use TensorFlow.js' visualization library **tfjs-vis** to see in real-time how the model's loss and performance metric evolve during training.

The evaluation phase also extends to the trained model. Here, we will test the model using data it did not see during the training phase to assess its predictive power. Doing so is very important because a model that does well at training is not necessarily good at predicting. One of the main reasons this phenomenon occurs is because of **overfitting**. An overfitted model is one that underwent a wrong training phase, and it *memorized*—instead of *modeled*—the training data, its noise, and random fluctuations. As a result, the model loses its ability to generalize, meaning that it will not work well in cases it did not see during the training.

Deploying the model

By this point, suppose we have a good model that fits the problem we defined right at the start. It did great during training and performs well on the testing phase, and your boss approves it. Now it is time to deploy and present it to the world. But how? This is neither an easy question to answer nor a trivial task to complete, because deploying a model depends on many factors, like the platform of interest or the company's requirements.

Deploying a model is the process of serving it or making it available for use. For example, Amazon's recommendation engines are probably located in Amazon Web Services servers, listening to our searches for "tensorflow js books." Typically, when we train machine learning models, we do it in an enclosed environment, like a script, a notebook, or a service somewhere in the cloud. However, the chances are that these are not the environments where you will deploy it. After all, these scripts might be designed for training and not for inferring. So, we need a second platform to deploy them.

As you might expect, our deployment target is TensorFlow.js—one that, as discussed earlier, performs well as a training and inferring platform.

To summarize this first part of the chapter, all the cases introduced here are a description and a guide on how you will approach most of this book's problems. Nevertheless, it is not an exhaustive or perfect list of how every machine learning system works. Now, let's finally apply all of this information and build the book's first models.

Building a logistic regression model

In this first exercise, we will create a web application that trains and serves a logistic regression model. Moreover, to have a richer application, we will use the visualization library tfjs-vis to plot the data and the training's loss and performance metric.

Since we are in a web environment, this tutorial also covers certain web development concepts such as loading libraries from a CDN or how to create a button dynamically. While these topics are not related to TensorFlow.js or ML, I believe that the book should explain them to understand the app thoroughly and to assist those who are not familiar with them.

Time to start! So, grab your laptop and prepare to get your hands dirty. Or, if you rather just read about the process, of course, that's great too. For extra references, you can find the complete source code at `https://github.com/Apress/Practical-TensorFlow.js/tree/master/2`.

Understanding logistic regression

This web app features a **logistic regression** (or logit) model, a supervised learning algorithm that tries to find an association between a set of **independent variables**, also known as the predictors, and a **discrete dependent variable**, known as the label. In other words, it uses a collection of attributes or features to learn to classify them into a category. The function that maps the set of features to the target is a special case of the logistic function (hence the name) called the sigmoid function.

Specifically speaking, the model in question is a **binary logistic regression model**, one whose target variable has one of **two** possible values, for example, "0" or "1," "true" or "false," or "spam" or "not spam." However, the algorithm's output does not look this way. A logit model's output is the likelihood or probability of the label being the default case. Let me explain. Suppose we have a model that predicts if a message is "spam" or "not spam," and we test it with the text: "TensorFlow.js is nice." The answer is, of course, "not spam," but the model won't say it this way. Instead, its output is a value between 0 and 1, where 1 means that it is 100% confident the message is spam, and 0 indicates that it is 0% likely to be spam. Typically, most implementations of logistic regression set the threshold at 0.5, meaning that they consider anything above this value the "true" response, for example, "spam," while anything below, the "false" one.

Figure 2-1 presents an example of a logistic function from a model that predicts a vehicle engine's shape (vs) where the label "0" means "V-shaped" and 1, "straight," using as predictor its horsepower (hp).[2] The dots you see here are the training set. In the x-axis, you have the horsepower, *hp*; in the y-axis, the engine's shape, *vs*; and in the chart, the logistic curve that maps both variables. To interpret it and to predict from this plot, consider the input *hp=100*. Now, go to the y-axis and find the value where "100" intercepts the "S" curve. In this case, it touches the curve in the 0.80 mark, and since 0.80 > 0.50, then the prediction is "1." On the other hand, if *hp=200*, the likelihood is 0.004, so the predicted label is "0."

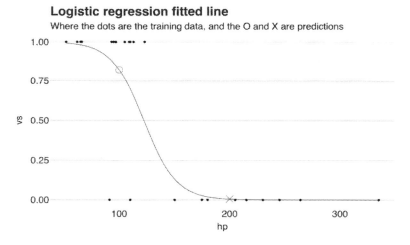

Figure 2-1. *A fitted logistic regression*

For this exercise, we will create a logistic regression using a network-like model in TensorFlow.js. But before getting there, we need to start by reviewing what an artificial neural network is.

---

[2]This is the classic *mtcars* dataset (Henderson & Velleman, 1981).

What is an artificial neural network?

Our brain is made of billions of interconnected neurons that are organized in a complex network-like structure. These neurons—the fundamental units of the brain—are continually sending electrical impulses, known as signals, that are received by others. Some signals are strong, and when they reach the receiving neuron, it stimulates them to create and transmit their own signal to the network. Weak signals, on the other hand, do not trigger an impulse.

An artificial neural network aims to mimic the connectivity and impulses characteristic of the brain. Its main block, the **perceptron** (Rosenblatt, 1958), plays the role of the biological neuron. A perceptron is a mathematical representation of the neuron, and like its biological counterpart, its role is to produce an output signal depending on whether the input was strong. It consists of five main parts and an additional one (Figure 2-2):

- Inputs: The incoming signals.

- Weights: Values that weigh (modify) the inputs. The weights are probably the most important part of the network. During training, the network will learn an optimal set of weights capable of producing the desired output.

- Weighted sum: This operation computes the weighted sum of the inputs $z = w_1x_1 + w_2x_2 + \ldots + w_nx_n$

- Activation function: This operation applies an activation function to the weighted sum.

- The output: This value is the activation function applied to the weighted sum $h_w(x) = activation(z)$; the outgoing signal.

- The bias (optional): Sometimes, a perceptron has an additional input called the bias, denoted with x_0. If bias is used, the weighted sum becomes $y = x_0 + w_1x_1 + w_2x_2 + \ldots + w_nx_n$.

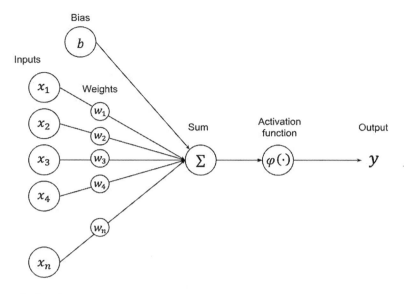

Figure 2-2. *A perceptron*

In one sentence, we could say that a perceptron is a structure that receives a series of inputs and produces an output. Let's see an example. Suppose that we have one perceptron with inputs $X_1 = 0.7$, $W_1 = 0.3$, $X_2 = 0.4$, $W_2 = 0$, and bias $X_0 = 1$, and the activation function is sigmoid (the one from logistic regression) defined as $\dfrac{1}{1+e^{-x}}$. In this case, the weighted sum is $y = 1 + 0.7 * 0.3 + 0.4 * 0 = 1.21$. And after applying the sigmoid activation function, $\dfrac{1}{1+e^{-1.21}} = 0.77$ (Figure 2-3).

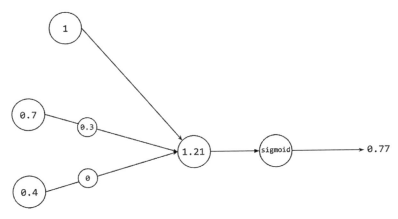

Figure 2-3. *An example of a perceptron with values*

Like the brain, in practice, you never use a single perceptron because one is not enough for learning complex problems. So, instead of using one, you use layers of perceptron that are connected, hence the term **artificial neural network** (ANN). An ANN has three kinds of layers: **input, hidden,** and **output** layers. The input layer receives the data and distributes it among the first hidden layer because, typically, the neurons of one layer are connected to all the neurons of the previous one, a *fully connected layer*. The hidden layers compute the activation values of their inputs and send them to the next one. Last, the output layer uses the activations from the past hidden layer to produce the final output. In a neural network architecture, the more layers you have, the more weights, increasing the network's capability of learning a solution to a more complex problem. For instance, the preceding example intends to learn only two weights. But in reality, a problem such as image classification could easily require a network of millions of weights. Therefore, to cope with the complexity, the network might require more layers.

But how do they learn? Excellent question. During training, the model tries to tweak its weight in such a way that it is able to predict the label of a dataset using its predictors. In our perceptron example, we used two predictors [0.7, 0.4], and the output was 0.7702. But what if the actual correct target is 1.0? Can we tweak the weights with the goal of getting a better output? The answer is yes.

During training, when a value reaches the output layer, the model calculates the difference between the actual and predicted values. This difference, formally known as the error, is sent back to the model's weight and bias to modify them in a way that minimizes the error; in other words, we update the weights to close the gap between the actual and predicted values. This process of sending the error back to the model is called **backpropagation** (Rumelhart et al., 1985). As we will soon see, a network learns in cycles known as **epochs**. At the end of each of these, the model propagates the errors back, with the intention of reducing the error in the upcoming epoch. So, you could see this as an iterative process that runs until the model finds an optimal set of weights or *converges*. As a result, it is not surprising to have a large error early during training. You will learn more about how the training error evolves through the visualizations we will create.

Overview of the data

This exercise's dataset is a synthetic one. It includes 700 observations, 2 features, and the class column named "label." It is balanced, with 349 points belonging to the class "0" and 351 to the second class, "1." Each of the features follows a normal distribution, meaning that most points are situated near the mean and have a standard deviation of 1. Besides this, to make the dataset suitable for a classification problem, the features are interdependent.

Building the app

For better visibility and clarity, we will split the tutorial into different sections, where each of them describes a particularity or a mechanism of the application. First, we will start by setting up the workspace, followed by defining the HTML file and importing the required packages. Then, we will load the dataset, plot it, and, last, build the model and train it. Follow me!

Setting up the workspace

For this exercise, the only thing you will need is a web browser and your preferred code editor. Nothing else. The app will use the CDN approach to download the libraries, so you do not have to install anything. Now, create a new project, open the code editor, and let's get started.

Structuring the HTML, importing the packages, and loading the script

In this first part of the tutorial, you will load both the TensorFlow.js and tfjs-vis packages via a CDN, define the structure and elements of the app using several HTML tags, and load the script that trains the model. But before doing all of that, please open your editor, create a new file, and name it *index.html*.

At the top of the file, create an <html> tag and the closing counterpart </html>. This essential tag is the element that represents the root of an HTML file. Next, within the tags, create a <head> tag—an element used to define metadata, styles, and scripts, among others—and close it. Then, inside the <head> tags, add the following lines to import TensorFlow.js and tfjs-vis:

```
<html>
    <head>
        <!-- Import TensorFlow.js -->
```

```
    <script src="https://cdn.jsdelivr.net/npm/@tensorflow/
    tfjs"></script>
    <!-- Import tfjs-vis -->
    script src="https://cdn.jsdelivr.net/npm/@tensorflow/
    tfjs-vis"></script>
  </head>
</html>
```

Next, right after the `</head>` line, create a `<body>` tag (within the `<html>` tags), which, as the name points out, defines the document's body and contains all its content.

The first element you will add in the body is a `<div>` tag, that is, a container or a division in an HTML document that encapsulates other elements. Inside this `<div>` tag, you will later add, programmatically using JS, the button that builds and displays the dataset's visualization. Therefore, set its `id` to `visualize`, like this:

```
<body>
    <div id="visualize"></div>
</body>
```

In the following line, add an `<input>` field of type "number," a blank space where the user can enter a number, hence the name input. In this field, the user will specify the number of training epochs, so use the id and name "number-epochs." Moreover, to make it more interesting, add a `min` attribute of value "1," a `max` attribute of value "20," and a default `value` set to "5." It should look like this:

```
<input type="number" id="number-epochs"
name="number-epochs" min="1" max="20" value="5" style="width: 5em">
```

Additionally, to improve the app's readability, add a `<label>` tag with the text "Number of epochs (between 1 and 20):" on top of the input:

```
<label for="number-epochs">Number of epochs (between 1 and 20):
</label>
<input type="number" id="number-epochs" name="number-epochs"
min="1" max="20" value="5" style="width: 5em">
```

The `<label>` tag improves the interaction and usability of the element we use it *for* (in this case, the input field) by highlighting the targeted element if the mouse is over the label or selecting it if the user clicks the label.

After the input, use a second `<div>` with the `id` attribute `train`. Like the previous `<div>`, in this one, the app adds the button that starts the model's training:

```
<div id="train"></div>
```

Last, add a `<script>` tag to import and run *index.js*, which is the script where you will write the web app's functionality. To import it, add the following line:

```
<script src="./index.js"></script>
```

And that's the first file. If everything went right (I'm sure it did), it should look like this:

```
<html>
<head>
    <!-- Import TensorFlow.js -->
    <script src="https://cdn.jsdelivr.net/npm/@tensorflow/tfjs">
    </script>
```

```
    <!-- Import tfjs-vis -->
    <script src="https://cdn.jsdelivr.net/npm/@tensorflow/
    tfjs-vis">
</script>
</head>
<body>
    <!-- The button that visualizes data goes here-->
    <div id="visualize"></div>
    <label for="number-epochs">Number of epochs (between 1 and 20):
    </label>
    <input type="number" id="number-epochs" name="number-
    epochs" min="1" max="20" value="5" style="width: 5em">
    <!-- The button to train the model goes here -->
    <div id="train"></div>
    <!-- Run index.js -->
    <script src="./index.js"></script>
</body>
</html>
```

To summarize, this HTML file is the skeleton of the app. In it, you have loaded the required libraries, defined its structure, and exported the JavaScript file that, in the next part, we will use to train a model with TensorFlow.js. So, before moving on, in the same directory where *index. html* is, create a new file and name it *index.js*.

Loading the data with TensorFlow.js Data (tfjs-data)

In this part of the tutorial, you will load the dataset that is required to train the model using tfjs-data. This component of TF.js provides the tools to load and parse data from both the Web and disk as well as to process it using operations such as *filter* and *shuffle*.

Before loading the dataset, first, you need to define its location, which, in this case, is a remote URL. So, in the first line of *index.js*, declare a variable and set its value to the following string (or you could copy the dataset from the book's repository):

```
const csvUrl =
   'https://gist.githubusercontent.com/juandes/ba58ef99df9bd71
   9f87f807e24f7ea1c/raw/59f57af034c52bd838c513563a3e547b3650e7
   ba/lr-dataset.csv';
```

Right under `csvUrl`, declare another one named `dataset`, the variable that will contain the dataset:

```
let dataset;
```

Next, create a function named `loadData()` to load the dataset and assign it to the variable `dataset` you just created. The function looks like this:

```
function loadData() {
  // Our target variable is the column 'label'
  dataset = tf.data.csv(
    csvUrl, {
      hasHeader: true,
      columnConfigs: {
        label: {
          isLabel: true,
        },
      },
    },
  );
}
```

Let's take a detailed look at what is happening here. Even though the function spreads across several lines, it only has one statement. That statement, or function to be more precise, is tf.data.csv() from tfjs-data. This function creates a CSVDataset object by reading and parsing a CSV file from a given URL passed as an argument. The function's second argument is a CSVConfig object, one that has several configurations about the file it is about to load.

In this case, the CSVConfig object has its hasHeader attribute set to true, indicating that the file's first row is a header line with the column's names and not data. Then, there is the columnConfigs attribute, a dictionary whose key is the column's name, and the value, an object of type ColumnConfig. Here, you will set the attribute isLabel of the column "label" (i.e., the name of the dataset's target variable) to true, to indicate that this column is the label and not another feature. If this specification is missing, the returned dataset is a dictionary of features only. Otherwise, like here, it is an object of the shape {xs: features, ys: labels}.

The attributes here presented are not the only ones supported by these objects. For instance, the CSVConfig object has a columnNames key which takes a list of strings that overrides the dataset column names.

In short, this command does the following:

1. First, it retrieves a dataset from a URL.

2. Then, it indicates that the dataset's first row is a header and not data.

3. It specifies that the column "label" is the target variable and not a feature.

Now that the data is here, let's proceed to visualize it.

Visualizing the data

In this part of the tutorial, you will use TensorFlow.js' visualization library, tfjs-vis, to plot the data. The plot is a scatter plot where the dataset's labels are displayed in different colors and shapes. A tfjs-vis visualization requires three main things: the **data**, a **visor**, and a **surface**. The data is self-explanatory. But, unlike other libraries, for example, R's *ggplot2*[3] and Python's *matplotlib*,[4] we can't just pass it as an argument and call it a day. So, as you will soon see, we have to pre-process it a bit. Then, there is the visor, a window that holds the surfaces, which are the tabs containing the charts. So, we have a visor with surfaces and surfaces with graphs (the data).

We will create the plot inside a function named `visualizeDataset()`. However, this won't be a standard function, but an **asynchronous** or async one. An async function is a function that does not follow the main execution thread of the program and, thus, runs asynchronously or separate from the main thread. These functions have many uses, but in this book, we will mostly use them to draw visualizations or load things in the background without blocking (freezing) the app:

```
async function visualizeDataset() {
}
```

Inside the function, declare two arrays, `classZero` and `classOne`. In `classZero`, you will add the dataset's features labeled with "0," and in `classOne`, the rows labeled with "1." Next, iterate over the dataset and check each row's label to add its features to the correct array. To do so, call

---

[3]https://ggplot2.tidyverse.org
[4]https://matplotlib.org

the dataset's method `forEachAsync()`, which asynchronously iterates over the dataset and applies a function to each of its elements. The following code snippet shows the process:

```
const classZero = [];
const classOne = [];
dataset.forEachAsync((e) => {
  // Extract the features from the dataset
  const features = {
    x: e.xs.feature_1,
    y: e.xs.feature_2,
  };
  if (e.ys.label == 0) {
    classZero.push(features);
  } else {
    classOne.push(features);
  }
});
```

In the loop's first line, create a variable named `features`, a dictionary of two keys, x and y, whose values are the first and the second feature of the dataset. Then, check if the label is "0." If true, push `features` to `classZero`. Otherwise, push it to `classOne`.

In its current state, the functions from `forEachAsync()` are executed asynchronously, meaning that the program continues its normal flow while they do their job somewhere else. On this occasion, we don't want to do this. Otherwise, the subsequent lines of code will execute while the functions might still be running. As a result, the program will suffer an unexpected behavior because the arrays `classZero` and `classOne` are not ready yet. So, we need to halt the execution until `forEachAsync()` ends. The way to do this is by adding the modifier `await` before calling the function. Among other things we will discover later, `await` causes the program to "suspend" its progress until the "awaited" statement finishes (it's like the program is saying "I'll wait until you're done." Cute).

Now, back in the main thread (no more talks about async and await), declare three new variables. The first of them, `series`, is a list of the names you want to give to the different labels in the chart's legend, for example, "Class 0" and "Class 1." The second one, `dataToDraw`, is a dictionary, and one of its keys, `values`, takes as value an array whose elements are {x, y} tuples (like the ones you added in the variable `features`). Then, the third one, `dataSurface`, is the surface we previously discussed. The surface is a dictionary with a key name which is the surface's name and a second key, `chart`, which indicates in which tab you want to draw the plot (if the tab does not exist, it creates one).

Lastly, you need to call the `tfvis.render.scatterplot()` function, the one responsible for drawing the chart. Its first parameter is the surface, followed by the data and an optional parameter `opts`, a dictionary with several configuration options. For this example, we are explicitly changing the name of both labels to "feature_1" and "feature_2" (this is not really necessary because that is the original name of the columns, but now we know how to do it) as well as setting `zoomToFit` to `true` to make the plot bounds to just fit the data. The following is the final function:

```
async function visualizeDataset() {
  const classZero = [];
  const classOne = [];

  await dataset.forEachAsync((e) => {
    // Extract the features from the dataset
    const features = {
      x: e.xs.feature_1,
      y: e.xs.feature_2,
    };
```

41

```
    if (e.ys.label === 0) {
      classZero.push(features);
    } else {
      classOne.push(features);
    }
  });
  const series = ['Class 0', 'Class 1'];
  const dataToDraw = {
    values: [classZero, classOne],
    series,
  };
  const dataSurface = {
    name: 'Scatterplot',
    tab: 'Charts',
  };
  tfvis.render.scatterplot(dataSurface, dataToDraw, {
    xLabel: 'feature_1',
    yLabel: 'feature_2',
    zoomToFit: true,
  });
}
```

There's an important detail the app is missing, and that's the functionality to call this function. Remember the <div> with ID visualize you added before? In the following steps, you will write a function named createVisualizeButton () that creates a button inside that <div>:

```
function createVisualizeButton() {
  const btn = document.createElement('BUTTON');
  btn.innerText = 'Visualize!';

  // Listener that waits for clicks. Once the
```

```
// button is clicked, it calls visualizeDataset
btn.addEventListener('click', () => {
  visualizeDataset();
});

// # is the ID selector. So it is searching
// for the element with id visualize.
document.querySelector('#visualize')
  .appendChild(btn);
}
```

In the first line, you will find a variable named btn and its value set to document.createElement('BUTTON'), a function that creates an instance of the specified HTML tag. Here, the returned element is a button (tag <button>). This statement does not imply that we now have a button in the app; the button exists but is not yet in the HTML. Still, you can work on it and even change its attributes. For instance, in the second line, the string "Visualize!" is being assigned to its attribute innerText. But attributes are not the only thing that you can add to the button.

Following the btn.innerText line, there is a statement involving the button's method addEventListener. This function sets up another one, known as the *listener*, that is triggered whenever the specified event happens. In this case, it is waiting or listening for a "click" event, meaning that when the user clicks the button, the listener executes. The listener you will use here is the visualizeDataset() function.

As for the last step, you will add the button to the document using the function document.querySelector(). This function takes as an argument a *selector*, which for this purpose means the ID of an element from the HTML file. Then, it returns the first element that matches the ID. As seen in the preceding code, the function's parameter is the "visualize" <div> you defined in the HTML. Once it returns the <div>, use the function appendChild() to append the button to it.

Defining the model

In this section, you will finally start working on the model, and the first task will be defining its architecture. Unlike other traditional machine learning libraries, in TensorFlow.js, we need to design the network, which means adding its layers, nodes, and configuration. Modeling a large network architecture is not a trivial task; it can confuse and is prone to mistakes. However, there are ways that simplify this procedure, and TensorFlow.js provides one: the Layers API and its `tf.Sequential` object.

Resuming the explanation started back in Chapter 1, a `tf.Sequential` object represents a set of layers, where the output of one is the input of the following one. In the case of the first layer, the shape of its input has to be defined. As for the others, TensorFlow.js infers their shape automatically. The layer we will use in this network, a dense layer, has three principal hyperparameters: **inputShape**, **units**, and **activation** function.

The first of these hyperparameters, *inputShape*, indicates the shape of the layer's input data. The second one, *units*, is a positive integer that describes the dimensionality of the output space. Last, we have *activation*, the activation function responsible for producing the layer's output.

This app's model contains a single layer responsible for computing the logistic function. To define the model, create a new async function named `defineAndTrainModel()`, with a parameter `numEpochs`. Next, inside the function, initialize a `tf.Sequential` model:

```
async function defineAndTrainModel(numEpochs) {
  const model = tf.sequential();
}
```

Inside the function, add a **dense** layer, the network's only layer using the method `model.add()`. A dense layer, also known as a fully connected layer, calculates the layer's output through the operation `output = activation(dot(input, weights) + bias)`, where *dot* is the dot product (matrix multiplication) of the input value and the layer's weights, and bias is the layer's bias vector. This layer's **input shape** is an array of length two, where each element is a feature of the dataset. Let's make a small pause here.

Since we know the dataset's number of features, we could simply write "2." But that is a bit ugly. Instead, let's use a more programmatic approach to obtain this number, namely, the dataset's method columnNames() to retrieve a list with the column names. Then, from that list, you can get its length by using the property length. After that, subtract 1 from the length since we do not want to count the label column. The statement looks like this:

```
const numFeatures = (await
  dataset.columnNames()).length - 1;
```

Notice the await keyword? The columnNames function is async, so to ensure that we have the value before continuing the execution, add an await. Back to the network.

The second hyperparameter of a dense layer is **units**, a value that defines the layer's output shape. When we discussed the logistic regression model, we stated that the model's output is a single number between 0 and 1. Such a number is of dimensionality one. So, set units to 1.

The last hyperparameter you will define is the activation function. On this occasion, the most appropriate one is the sigmoid function, a special case of the general logistic function and the one used in the logistic regression algorithm. The following code shows the defined layer:

```
// Add a Dense layer to the Sequential model
 model.add(tf.layers.dense({
    inputShape: [numFeatures],
    units: 1,
    activation: 'sigmoid',
 }));
```

As for the final step before starting the training, you have to compile the model using the method `compile()` to configure and prepare the model. This function takes as an argument a `ModelCompileArgs` object that specifies the training optimizer, loss function, and evaluation metric. For this model, use the following configuration:

- The Adam **optimizer**, an efficient optimization algorithm that computes individual learning rates (how fast a particular weight is updated) for each weight of the neural network (Kingma & Ba, 2014).

- The binary cross-entropy **loss** function, a function that measures how far a prediction outcome is from its real value and then averages these differences or errors to obtain one value. This value is the loss.

- The accuracy **metric**, a score that measures the fraction or ratio of predictions the model correctly guessed.

The following is the model's compile statement and the complete function:

```
async function defineAndTrainModel(numEpochs) {
  const model = tf.sequential();

  const numFeatures = (await
    dataset.columnNames()).length - 1;

  // Add a Dense layer to the Sequential model
  model.add(tf.layers.dense({
    inputShape: [numFeatures],
    units: 1,
    activation: 'sigmoid',
  }));
```

```
model.compile({
  optimizer: tf.train.adam(0.1),
  loss: 'binaryCrossentropy',
  metrics: ['accuracy'],
});
}
```

Training and visualizing the training

Now that the model is defined, and compiled, the next step before training it involves changing the dataset's structure to make it suitable for the `model.fitDataset()` method, the one that trains the model. By this point, the dataset is a list where each element is a dictionary of two keys: xs and ys. The key's xs value is another dictionary where the keys are the names of the features, and the value is the feature itself. The second key, ys, is also a dictionary of only one key, label, whose value is the row's class. The next line shows an example.

```
[{xs: {feature_1: 0.23, feature_2: -1.90},
  ys: {label: 1},
 {xs: {feature_1: 1.83, feature_2: 0.73},
  ys: {label: 0},
 {...}, ... {...}]
```

As readable as it is for us (right?), this format won't work for training the model. So, you have to change a few things, starting with removing the nested dictionaries. Then, extract the features and the label values, and add them to two separate arrays. Afterward, add these two arrays to a dictionary with a key xs that holds the flattened features and another key ys that has as value the label. So, in the end, the dataset will look like this:

```
[{xs: [0.23, -1.90], ys: [1]},
 {xs: [1.83, -0.73],  ys: [0]}]
```

To change the data to this format, use the dataset's method map(). This method executes a function on each row of the dataset to get the values of the dictionaries xs and ys and convert them into the desired format. The following is the code. Write it under the model.compile() line from defineAndTrainModel().

```
// Convert the features (xs) and labels (ys) to an
// array
const flattenedDataset = dataset
  .map(({ xs, ys }) => ({
    xs: Object.values(xs),
    ys: Object.values(ys),
  }))
  .batch(10)
  .shuffle(100, 1717); // buffer size and seed
```

See those two functions, batch() and shuffle()? The first one, batch(), groups the data into chunks of *N* samples. Usually, using smaller batches leads to a training that requires less memory, because the network trains using fewer samples. Also, it might even train faster because the network's weights are updated after each batch, and not after assessing the whole dataset. On the other hand, since the network is evaluating less data, it might not be as accurate as one done without batching. The second function, shuffle(), shuffles the dataset using a streaming approach by sampling *N* (the first parameter) elements and shuffling those; the second parameter is the seed for reproducibility.

Now, for real this time, let's train the model using model.fitDataset(). This function is asynchronous, so like before we will use an await modifier. The method model.fitDataset() takes two parameters, a tf.data.Dataset like the one you have already prepared and a ModelFitDatasetArgs object with several fields we will describe next.

The ModelFitDatasetArgs object you will use has two keys: epochs and callbacks. The first one, epochs, corresponds to the training's number of epochs. Set it to numEpochs. Then, there is the callback key, which takes a list of callback functions that executes at several stages of the training. For this model, you will use the following two callbacks:

- onTrainEnd(logs): Callback called when the training ends; the parameter logs contain logs about the training. It is used here to print to the console "training has ended" when the training ends.

- onEpochEnd(epoch, logs): Callback called at the end of every epoch. The parameter epoch refers to the epoch's number. logs is an object that has the loss function's current value and the evaluation metrics. It is used here to print the loss value at the end of every epoch.

Besides these uses, we will use the callbacks to visualize in real-time the training's loss and the performance metric. The tfjs-vis library provides a function, tfvis.show.fitCallbacks(), that returns a collection of callback functions you can directly pass to the callbacks of model.fitDataset(). This function takes as arguments a surface, a list of the metrics to display, and an optional configuration object. In the configuration object, we will use the callbacks property to specify that we want to update the charts at the end of every epoch. With that, we conclude the training code. The following is the complete fitDataset() statement (add it after the variable flattenedDataset).

```
await model.fitDataset(flattenedDataset, {
    epochs: numEpochs,
    callbacks: [
      tfvis.show.fitCallbacks(
        { name: 'Loss and MSE', tab: 'Training' },
        ['loss', 'acc'],
        { callbacks: ['onEpochEnd'] },
      ),
```

```
    {
      onEpochEnd: async (epoch, logs) => {
        console.log(`${epoch}:${logs.loss}`);
      },
    },
    {
      onTrainEnd: async () => {
        console.log('Training has ended.');
      },
    }],
  });
```

And that's how you train a model! To quickly summarize, here we have created a `tf.Sequential` object of one layer, compiled it, and ultimately trained it. Now, please make sure you closed the `defineAndTrainModel()` function.

Wrapping things up and running the app

The code is missing two things: a way to start the training and reading the `number-epochs` input from the HTML. To do this, as before, you will programmatically create a button in the `train` `<div>` with a listener that initiates the training once the user clicks it. In this same listener, you will read the value from the `number-epochs` input field using `document.getElementById()` and its property, `value`. Then, to ensure the value is an integer, convert it to a number, and finally, pass it to `defineAndTrainModel ()`:

```
function createTrainButton() {
  const btn = document.createElement('BUTTON');
  btn.innerText = 'Train!';

  btn.addEventListener('click', () => {
```

```
  const numberEpochs = document.getElementById('number-
  epochs').value;
  // The 10 indicates the number is in base 10.
  defineAndTrainModel(parseInt(numberEpochs, 10));
});

document.querySelector('#train').appendChild(btn);
}
```

After that, create an init() function and call it:

```
function init() {
  createTrainButton();
  createVisualizeButton();
  loadData();
}
```

```
init();
```

Congratulations! You just finished your first TensorFlow.js application. To run it, go to your computer's file manager (*Finder* on Mac or *File Explorer* on Windows), and double-click the *index.html* file to open the web app in your default web browser.

In the app, you should see the "Visualize!" button. If you click it, the tfvis visor shows up on the right side of the screen. There you will find the scatter plot of the data and its two classes. One of them, class "0," is at the bottom of the graph and class "1" in the top-center region. Since there is a clear gap between both classes (except for the minimal noise), the model should be able to find the separation quickly.

Similarly, you will see the training button and the "number of epochs" input field with its default value of 5. After changing the value (or not), click the button to begin the training. Right after clicking, the visualization visor switches to the *Training* tab to present the real-time charts of the loss value and accuracy. Oh, if you wish to close (or open) the visor, press the backtick key.

Training with five epochs is a bit exaggerated. If you see the graphs, you will realize that the loss and accuracy values do not change that much (Figure 2-4). It only took one epoch to achieve an accuracy of over 93%!

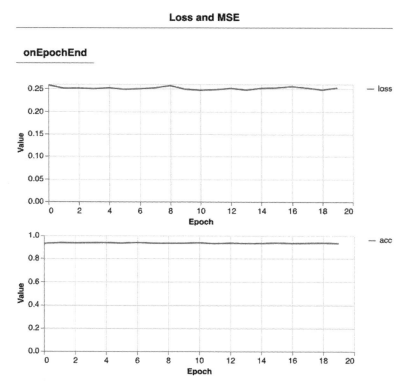

Figure 2-4. *Loss and accuracy values*

There is one crucial thing this exercise is missing, and that's using the model to predict an outcome. To predict, call the method `model.predict()` using as input a tensor of the same shape as the one used for training. The tensor's values are the predictors, the input data we want to classify. In this case, since we have a synthetic dataset, there is no real meaning behind the predictors. In the following are some examples of how to predict using some arbitrary values. You can add these lines anywhere after `model.fitDataset()`:

```
// Output value should be near 0.
model.predict(tf.tensor2d([[0.1773208878849,
  -1.447465411302]])).print();

// Output value should be near 1.
model.predict(tf.tensor2d([[-1.58566906881,
  1.91762229933]])).print();
```

In the first example, the prediction value should be close to 0, that is, 0.0613599, meaning that we should classify this case with the label "0." The second example outputs a number close to 1, so its label is "1" since it is above the usual threshold of 0.5.

Recap

In this first exercise, you have built and trained your first TensorFlow.js model, a logistic regression. During the tutorial, we explored essential concepts of TensorFlow.js, such as loading a dataset, preparing it, designing a model, and training it. Moreover, we also used TensorFlow.js' visualization library, tfjs-vis, to visualize the dataset and monitor training.

In the following section, we will introduce a second model, linear regression, to create a model that predicts a continuous value.

Building a linear regression model

In the previous section, we explored the basic components of TensorFlow. js and used them to develop a logistic regression model. In this exercise, we will keep building on that knowledge and implement another model in a second web application. This time, the algorithm in question is linear regression, a supervised learning algorithm that predicts a scalar response. We will use it to create a model capable of predicting the distance the author would walk in one day, given the number of taken steps.

The web app you will develop follows a similar approach to the one we just did. It downloads a dataset, processes it, plots it with tfjs-vis, and then fits a model with it. But, in this one, you will create a mechanism that allows the user to enter a value (number of steps) to predict an outcome using the model.

Understanding linear regression

Linear regression is one of the most useful and essential tools from machine learning and statistics. Its objective is modeling an association between a set of independent variables and a target continuous variable—a variable whose value can be any number between a minimum and a maximum value—by finding a linear equation, short for just a line, that best fits the data.

Let's see a fun example. In Figure 2-5, you can find a scatter plot showing the *Hit Points* (HP) and *Combat Power* (CP) of a sample of *Pidgey* (a Pokémon) from the game *Pokémon Go*.[5] Now suppose we want to know the HP of a Pidgey whose CP stat is 100. How do we do this? With a linear regression model!

---

[5]*Pokémon, Pokémon Go*, and Pokémon names are trademarks of Nintendo.

Figure 2-6 shows the same dataset, but with a fitted line that serves to predict the Pokémon's CP using its HP as the independent variable. If you look at the upper-right corner of the graph, you will find our test case (HP = 100) and the model's output (CP = 40.9) marked with a big dot.

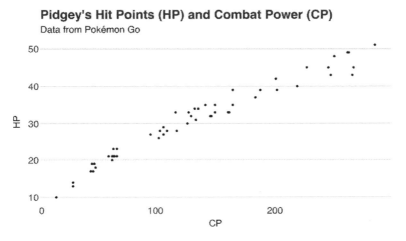

Figure 2-5. *Sample of Pidgey's HP and CP*

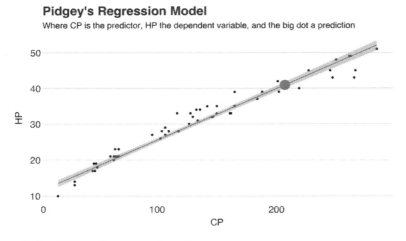

Figure 2-6. *Pidgey's regression line*

There are two things that we need to notice here. Unlike the previous logistic regression model, linear regression predicts a continuous value, which in this example could have been any number from 0 up to plus infinity. Moreover, we also need to be aware that linear regression works on the assumption that there is a linear relationship between the independent variables and the dependent variable. Otherwise, if the dataset does not meet this assumption, then the model's predictive power will be highly inaccurate.

For example, Figure 2-7 shows the population of Puerto Rico from the year 1960 until 2018 and a suboptimal regression line that does not fully fit the dataset. Until the 2000s, the population increase was mostly linear. After that, it starts to decline and loses its linearity. Yet, the regression line keeps growing. So, this model is not useful.

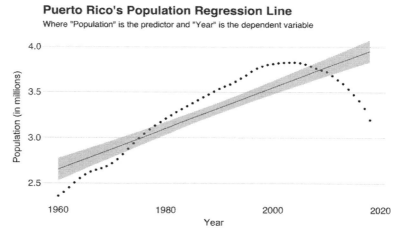

Figure 2-7. *A bad regression*

Overview of the data

The data you will use to train the model is a small dataset of 198 observations, where each row represents a particular day. It has two columns: the number of steps walked in that day and the total distance (in kilometers) traveled. Since the goal here is predicting the distance walked based on steps taken, the former plays the role of the dependent variable and the latter, the independent variable. In contrast to the last exercise's synthetic dataset, this one comes from the author's Fitbit[6] device.

Building the app

You will build this app following a similar approach to the last one. In the beginning, you will set up the workspace. Once set, we will discuss how to structure the HTML and import the necessary packages. After this part, you will load and plot the dataset, followed by defining the model and training it. Then, we will end this tutorial by building a feature for the app that will let the user make predictions from it.

Setting up the workspace

For reasons covered in the following segment, you will host the web application in a local web server. But do not despair; it is not as hard as it sounds. Chances are you have Python installed in your machine. If so, starting a local HTTP server is only a matter of executing `python3 -m http.server` in the terminal. But since this book is about a web framework, it makes more sense to use something along those lines to create the server. So, as an alternative to Python, you could use *http-server*,[7] a command-line HTTP server. To install it, execute `npm install http-server -g` (you need to have Node.js installed in your computer). To start the server, run `http-server`. By default, it runs the server on port 8080, but you can change it using the `-p` or `--port` option.

---

[6]Fitbit is a registered trademark and service mark of Fitbit, Inc.
[7]`www.npmjs.com/package/http-server`

Now create the project's directory on the location of your preference, and in the terminal, navigate to that folder. Once there, execute the previous command to start the server.

To test it, create a new file in the project's directory, name it *index. html*, and write "hello, world" on it. Then, open a new browser tab and go to localhost:8080 (make sure the port number is the correct one). You should see a page with the message you wrote. Now, let's turn this page into something better.

Structuring the HTML, importing the packages, and loading the script

Still on the same HTML file? Good, because you will need it. In this step, you will define the structure of the app's interface and load TensorFlow.js and tfjs-vis and the training script. But first, remove the "hello, world" line you previously wrote.

Afterward, create the root <html> tag, and within it, add a <head> tag (do not forget to close them!). Inside the <head> tag, add the script tags to import TensorFlow.js and tfjs-vis:

```
<script src="https://cdn.jsdelivr.net/npm/@tensorflow/tfjs">
</script>
<script src="https://cdn.jsdelivr.net/npm/@tensorflow/tfjs-vis">
</script>
```

In the line that follows the </head> tag, create a <body> tag. Like the last exercise, inside this node you will define elements whose content is programmatically created by the app. The first of these elements is a <div> with id attribute load-plot. Within this <div>, the program creates a button that, once clicked, loads and plots the dataset.

Right after it, add an input field of type "number," with ID number-epochs. Like last time, you will use this field to specify for how many epochs you want to train the model. On this occasion, let's avoid adding a maximum value; have fun and play around with the model (break it if you want!). On top of this input field, add a <label> element. Set the for attribute to the same ID as the input. Then, after the input, create another <div> with id attribute train-div. Here, the app will create the button that starts the training.

There is a third and more interesting <div> section that we will use for the app's prediction functionality. Within this node, we will have three elements. The most important of them is a numeric input field that the user will use to enter the value the model uses to predict. Next, there is a button that once clicked reads the input value and triggers the prediction. Lastly, the final element is a paragraph <p> that displays the model's output.

Last but not least, add the script tag that calls the *index.js* script. The following code shows the complete *index.html* file:

```html
<html>
<head>
    <script src="https://cdn.jsdelivr.net/npm/@tensorflow/
    tfjs"></script>
    <script src="https://cdn.jsdelivr.net/npm/@tensorflow/
    tfjs-vis"></script>
</head>
<body>
    <div id="load-plot"></div>
    <label for="number-epochs">Epochs</label>
    <input type="number" id="number-epochs" name="number-
    epochs" min="1" value="5" style="width: 5em">
    <div id="train-div"></div>
    <div id="predict"></div>
    <script src="./index.js"></script>
</body>
</html>
```

If the server is still up, go again to the browser and refresh the page so you can see how your masterpiece app is shaping up.

Loading and visualizing the data with tfjs-data and tfjs-vis

Close *index.html* and say hello to *index.js*. This part of the exercise is about loading the data using tfjs-data and visualizing it with tfjs-vis. So, as the first step, declare the variable csvUrl at the top of the file and set its value to the dataset's remote location. After that, declare a second variable and name it csvDataset.

In this example, we will do things a bit differently than the previous one. Instead of plotting just the training set, we will also plot the test cases from several parts of the app. So, we need several arrays that will contain the data to draw. In addition to them, declare the tfjs-vis' surfaces:

```
const csvUrl = 'https://gist.githubusercontent.com/juandes/
2f1ffa32dd4e58f9f5825eca1806244b/raw/c5b387382b162418f051fd83d
89fddb4067b91e1/steps_distance_df.csv';
let csvDataset;
const dataSurface = {
  name: 'Steps and Distance Scatterplot',
  tab: 'Data' };
const fittedSurface = {
  name: 'Fitted Dataset', tab: 'Data' };
const dataToVisualize = [];
const predictionsToVisualize = [];
let fittedLinePoints = [];
```

Following this, create the plotting function and call it loadData(). This function has to be async because it uses the forEachAsync() method we used earlier to iterate over the data and change its structure:

```
async function loadData() {
  csvDataset = tf.data.csv(
    csvUrl, {
      columnConfigs: {
        distance: {
          isLabel: true,
        },
      },
    },
  );

  await csvDataset.forEachAsync((e) => {
    dataToVisualize.push({
      x: e.xs.steps,
      y: e.ys.distance,
    });
  });

  tfvis.render.scatterplot(dataSurface, {
    values: [dataToVisualize],
    series: ['Dataset'],
  });
}
```

The function's first statement loads the data (the dataset is also available in the book's repository) and stores it in the csvDataset variable you previously declared. In the line that proceeds, we iterate over the dataset using forEachAsync(), and in each iteration, create a dictionary made of two keys, x and y. Set the value of x to the number of steps and the value of y to the distance. These dictionaries are then pushed to dataToVisualize. After forEachAsync(), call tfvis.render.scatterplot() using as arguments the surface dataSurface and an object consisting of the values to visualize and the series.

By this point, you might be wondering, "what if I want to load a dataset not from the Internet, but from a local directory, can I do this?" The answer is yes! You can do so with the same tf.data.csv() function by specifying the path to the local file, instead of a URL. But there is a small catch, and it is that the app must be running on a web server. Otherwise, you will meet an error due to a mechanism called **same-origin policy** and **cross-origin resource sharing** (CORS).

For the sake of clarification, we could say that the same-origin policy is a security mechanism that denies one document loaded from one origin to load another from another origin. CORS, on the other hand, is the tool that enables resource sharing across origins. In the case of running a web app directly from the HTML (like we did in the first exercise), Internet browsers restrict access to other local files. Contrarily, an application running on a server has no issues accessing a file that is also in the server. If you wish to use a local version of the dataset, save the remote one locally or get it from the book's repository. Then, back at the code, replace the dataset's URL with steps_distance_df.csv.

After loadData(), define createLoadPlotButton(), the function that calls it:

```
function createLoadPlotButton() {
  const btn = document.createElement('BUTTON');
  btn.innerText = 'Load and plot data';
  btn.id = 'load-plot-btn';

  btn.addEventListener('click', () => {
    loadData();
  });

  document.querySelector('#load-plot')
    .appendChild(btn);
}
```

This function works just like the one we used in the past section. It creates a button with a listener that runs loadData() once it receives a click. To end the section, create the init() function that calls createLoadPlotButton():

```
function init() {
  createLoadPlotButton();
}
```

```
init();
```

Return to the app and click the button to load and plot the data. Everything worked, right? There you should see the data and its linearly characteristic (just what linear regression likes!), which honestly is not that surprising at all because my walking stride is quite constant. Remember that you can close and open the visor by pressing the backtick key.

Defining the model

Now that we have the data, we will proceed to define the model. So, let's open this section by declaring the model's variable, model, at the top of the file. Then, create a new async function named defineAndTrainModel() with a parameter numEpochs (does this process sound familiar?). At the top of the function, use tfvis.visor().open() to force open the visualization visor. After this line, use const numFeatures = (await csvDataset. columnNames()).length - 1 to create a variable with the number of features as well as a map() operation on csvDataset to create a flattened version of the dataset.

```
let model;
```

```
async function defineAndTrainModel(numEpochs) {
  // Make sure the tfjs-vis visor is open.
  tfvis.visor().open();
```

```
const numFeatures = (await csvDataset.columnNames())
  .length - 1;

// Convert the features (xs) and labels (ys) to an array
const flattenedDataset = csvDataset
  .map(({ xs, ys }) => ({ xs: Object.values(xs), ys: Object.
  values(ys) }))
  .batch(32);
}
```

Now comes the fun part, and that's designing the model. Once again, it has a single layer with one unit (it gets better later; I promise). To design it, create an instance of tf.Sequential and set it to the model variable you just defined. After that, add a dense layer to the model and pass as argument a dictionary with key inputShape set to [numFeatures], and units set to 1. This latter value is 1 because we expect the model's output to be a single number representing the predicted distance. Also, note that we are not using an activation function because we want to model a linear relationship between the inputs and output:

```
model = tf.sequential();
model.add(tf.layers.dense({
  inputShape: [numFeatures],
  units: 1,
}));
```

Following the model's definition, the next step is compiling it and setting its optimizer, loss function, and metric score. In this occasion, you will use the following parameters:

- **Adam** optimizer.

- The **mean squared error** (MSE) loss function, a function that measures the mean of the squares of the errors, that is, the difference between the actual label and the predicted one, that is, $loss = (y_{true} - y_{pred})^2$. Remember that during training, the model wants this number to be as low as possible.

- As for the last parameter, the metric score, this model also uses the **mean squared error**.

```
model.compile({
    optimizer: tf.train.adam(0.1),
    loss: tf.losses.meanSquaredError,
    metrics: ['mse'], // Also mean squared error
});
```

Lastly, call model.fitDataset() using flattenedDataset as the first argument. For the second argument, use an object whose values are the numEpochs variable and a list of callback functions that are executed at several stages of the training. For this model, use only one callback function to visualize the training loss and MSE metric at the end of each epoch (onEpochEnd).

There is a new thing I want us to do with model.fitDataset(), and that's using its returned value. Back when we introduced the await keyword, we described it as a mechanism used for waiting for an asynchronous function to finish its execution. While true, the technical explanation is that it waits until the async function returns something known as a **promise**. A promise is a programming pattern that refers to a value that returns sometime in the future. In other words, an await statement causes the program to stop and wait for what was promised.

An async function always returns an implicit promise that supplies the intended value—the return value you specified—at some point in the future (if the function has no return line, the promise intended value is void). In the case of model.fitDataset(), it returns a "promised" *History*, formally written as *Promise<History>*. A History object is essentially a record of the training's loss and metric values at each epoch, information that might be valuable if one wishes to further evaluate the model. For this example, we will just print it:

```
const history = await
  model.fitDataset(flattenedDataset, {
    epochs: numEpochs,
    callbacks: [
      tfvis.show.fitCallbacks(
        { name: 'Loss and MSE', tab: 'Training' },
        ['loss', 'mse'],
        { callbacks: ['onEpochEnd'] },
      ),
      {
        onEpochEnd: async (epoch, logs) => {
          console.log(`${epoch}:${logs.loss}`);
        },
      }],
  });
  console.log(history);
```

Now, close defineAndTrainModel() (we will come back to it later). Before wrapping up this section, implement the function that creates the button that starts the training. This function is very similar to the one also defined here, except for one detail. By default, the function disables the button so that we cannot start the training until the data is loaded:

```
function createTrainButton() {
  const btn = document.createElement('BUTTON');
  btn.innerText = 'Train!';
  btn.disabled = true;
  btn.id = 'train-btn';
```

```
btn.addEventListener('click', () => {
  const numberEpochs =
    document.getElementById('number-epochs').value;
  defineAndTrainModel(parseInt(numberEpochs, 10));
});

document.querySelector('#train-div')
  .appendChild(btn);
}
```

That button is to stay disabled until the user loads the data. To enable it back, return to `createLoadPlotButton()`, and after the call to `loadData()` (in the listener), add the following two lines:

```
const trainBtn = document
  .getElementById('train-btn');
trainBtn.disabled = false;
```

The first instruction gets the button by its ID, while the second one sets its `disabled` attribute to `false`.

Once done, go to the `init()` function and call `createTrainButton()` from the first line. Then, test the app. Is it running yet? Good. There you should see two buttons, "load and plot" data and the disabled "train." Click the first one to load and visualize the data. After clicking it, the grayed-out button should now be enabled. So, click it to train the model.

For this model, I recommend training for around 20 epochs. Plus, the training phase is so fast that 1 or 20 epochs do not make that much of a difference. When it finishes, open the inspect tab from the browser to see the model's History.

One interesting thing we could do with the model is showing the fitted line it learns, like in Figure 2-6. Unfortunately, with our current tools, there is no direct way of doing this. But there is a very hacky one. This approach involves performing many predictions using as input a sequence of incremental values (this is usually known as "range") and plotting these values and the output produced by the model. For our dirty experiment, we could use 0 as the minimum and 30,000 as maximum with an increment step of 500 (this would give us 61 points). Let's try this with the following function:

```
function drawFittedLine(min, max, steps) {
  // Empty the array in case the user trains more than once.
  fittedLinePoints = [];
  const predictors = Array.from(
    { length: (max - min) / steps + 1 },
    (_, i) => min + (i * steps),
  );

  const predictions = model
    .predict(tf.tensor1d(predictors))
    .dataSync();

  predictors.forEach((value, i) => {
    fittedLinePoints
      .push({ x: value, y: predictions[i] });
  });

  const structureToVisualize = {
    values: [dataToVisualize, fittedLinePoints],
    series: ['1. Training Data', '2. Fitted Line'],
  };

  tfvis.render.scatterplot(fittedSurface,
    structureToVisualize);
}
```

Then, add a call to `drawFittedLine()` after the line that prints the model's History using the current parameters:

```
drawFittedLine(0, 30000, 500);
```

To test this functionality, restart the app, and train again. In my case, I trained using 15 epochs, producing the loss and error graph seen in Figure 2-8. Unlike our previous loss graph, in this one, you can clearly see how the loss function goes from a large value early during training to a low one. When the training ends, switch to the visor's "Training," and there you will find both the training data and the fitted line in separate plots. Try different epoch values to see how the line evolves (the sweet spot is around 40–50 epochs). Figure 2-9 presents a screenshot of the plot.

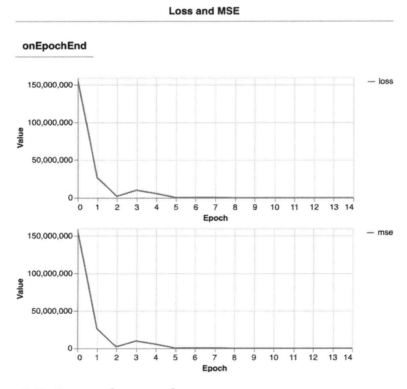

Figure 2-8. *Loss and error values*

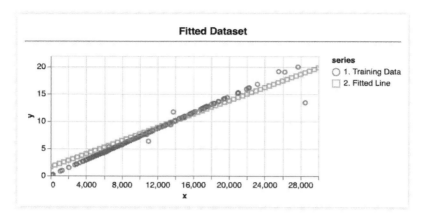

Figure 2-9. *Training set (circles) and the fitted line (squares)*

Testing the model

To have a more complete and useful application, you will implement a feature that allows a user to enter a value—the number of steps—to predict the distance I would walk on a day. To build such functionality, you will create an input field and a click button that, when pressed, parses the value and predicts with it. After predicting, the app draws the input data and the prediction so we can visually assess the accuracy. Lastly, the outcome is displayed on the app's <p> tag mentioned earlier. In the following, you will find the functions that create the input field createPredictionInput(), the output paragraph createPredictionOutputParagraph(), and the button createPredictButton().

First is createPredictionInput():

```
function createPredictionInput() {
  const input = document.createElement('input');
  input.type = 'number';
  input.id = 'predict-input';
```

```
  document
    .querySelector('#predict').appendChild(input);
}
```

Now `createPredictionOutputParagraph()`:

```
function createPredictionOutputParagraph() {
  const p = document.createElement('p');
  p.id = 'predict-output-p';

  document.querySelector('#predict').appendChild(p);
}
```

And `createPredictButton()`:

```
function createPredictButton() {
  const btn = document.createElement('BUTTON');
  btn.innerText = 'Predict!';
  btn.disabled = true;
  btn.id = 'predict-btn';

  btn.addEventListener('click', () => {
    // Get the value from the input
    const valueToPredict = document
      .getElementById('predict-input').value;
    const parsedValue = parseInt(valueToPredict, 10);
    const prediction = model
      .predict(tf.tensor1d([parsedValue]))
      .dataSync();

    // Get the <p> element and append the prediction
    const p = document
      .getElementById('predict-output-p');
    p.innerHTML = `Predicted value: ${prediction}`;
```

```
    // Push the input and prediction to
    // predictionsToVisualize. Then, draw it.
    predictionsToVisualize.push(
      { x: parsedValue, y: prediction },
    );
    const structureToVisualize = {
      values: [dataToVisualize, predictionsToVisualize],
      series: ['1. Training Data', '2. Predictions'],
    };

    tfvis.render.scatterplot(dataSurface, structureToVisualize);
    // Automatically switch to the "Data" tab
    tfvis.visor().setActiveTab('Data');
  });
  document.querySelector('#predict').appendChild(btn);
}
```

As before, you will notice that the "predict" button is disabled. To enable it, add the next two lines below drawFittedLine() in defineAndTrainModel():

```
const predictBtn = document.getElementById('predict-btn');
predictBtn.disabled = false;
```

Next, add the three functions to init(), run the app, and predict. You will notice that after predicting, the visor switches to the "Data" tab and shows on the first chart the input value and the outcome.

```
function init() {
  createTrainButton();
  createPredictionInput();
  createPredictButton();
  createPredictionOutputParagraph();
  createLoadPlotButton();
}
```

Explaining the model

One last thing we will do in this exercise is interpreting the model to know why it predicts the way it does. Before breaking it down, we will use the method `model.summary()` to review the model's layers and parameters. These parameters, also known as weights, are the things the model learns; learning in ML is finding a good set of weights. So, with the weight's values, we can reconstruct the equation the model learned from the data.

Back when we introduced the linear regression algorithm, we mentioned that its objective is finding a line that best fits the data. Straight lines, and maybe you remember this from school, are described by the following equation: $y = mx + b$, where m is the slope (how steep the line is) and b is the y-intercept (the value of y when $x = 0$). These two variables are what the model is trying to learn.

If you execute `model.summary()` at some point after the training, it outputs a table such as the one in Figure 2-10.

Layer (type)	Output shape	Param #
dense_Dense1 (Dense)	[null,1]	2

Total params: 2
Trainable params: 2
Non-trainable params: 0

Figure 2-10. *The model's summary*

On the first column, you have the dense layer, followed by its output shape and a column "param" which counts how many parameters the layer has—two. To get them and print them, add this line after `model.summary()`:

```
console.log(`Model weights:\n${model.getWeights()}`);
```

The values that follow are the model's weights after training it for 45 epochs (you might get a slightly different result):

```
Model weights:
Tensor
[[0.0007682],],Tensor
[-0.6309097]
```

The first number, 0.0007682, is the weight of the layer's only node—this value is the equivalent to the line's slope m. The second number, -0.6309097, is the node's bias, and it represents the regression line's y-intercept. Thus, to conclude, if we insert these numbers in the line equation, it will look as follows: $y = 0.0007682x + -0.6309097$, where x is the number of steps and y, the predicted distance. To manually test it, try the equation with $x = 1000$.

$$\left(0.0007682 * 1000\right) + -0.6309097 = 0.137290$$

This result means 1000 footsteps equal 0.13 kilometers traversed. To test the result (no, I'm not going to send you running), return to the app, and make a prediction also using 1000 as input. The result should be similar to the previous one.

Recap

In this example, we developed a web app that trains a linear regression, an algorithm that seeks to find a line that fits a dataset to predict a continuous outcome. The model we built uses steps data to predict distance walked. Through this exercise, we learned how to use tfjs-data to retrieve data from a local file, how to interpret a model, and how to read a user's input to predict.

Wrapping things up

Over the last two exercises, we have explored the fundamental structures of TensorFlow.js to fit a logistic and linear regression model using the Layers API. As part of the training, we used two additional components of TF.js to handle the data and to visualize it. The first of these, tfjs-data, is a module for loading and processing data, while the second, tfjs-vis, provides a simple API for visualizing data and aspects of the training. Additionally, earlier in the chapter, we saw a guide on how to approach a machine learning problem, and throughout the tutorials, we applied most of the guide's content. For instance, we explored the data, defined the model's architecture, and tested it.

What we saw here is a preview of what we can achieve with TensorFlow.js. While most applications follow the same method and employ the same techniques and functions, the extent of what they can do goes further than what we have done so far. In the next and upcoming chapters, we will keep exploring and using the framework to develop more exciting and powerful apps.

The complete source code of both apps is available on the book's GitHub page. The version of the app you will find there contains part of the documentation here discussed and a CSS file to improve the app's looks.

EXERCISES

1. What are the three principal hyperparameters a model uses?

2. Re-train all of them using other datasets. Chapter 11 tells more about where to find them.

3. What is the main difference between logistic and linear regression?

4. Want to see two examples of models gone wrong? Train both
    models using each other's datasets. This will give you an idea
    on the importance of choosing an appropriate loss function.

5. Fit another logistic and linear regression model using a
    generated dataset created with tf.data.generator()
    like this:

```
function* data() {
  for (let i = 0; i < 100; i++) {
    yield tf.tensor1d([1]);
  }
}

function* labels() {
  for (let i = 0; i < 100; i++) {
    yield tf.tensor1d([1]);
  }
}

const xs = tf.data.generator(data);
const ys = tf.data.generator(labels);
const ds = tf.data.zip({ xs, ys }).batch(32);
```

Then, use ds as the first argument of model.fitDataset(). Try
different combinations of tensor's values. This sample produces a
dataset where the features and labels are 1; not interesting at all.

6. In the linear regression model, use the property weights of the
    dense layers to set the weights.

CHAPTER 3

Doing k-means with ml5.js

In the last chapter, we explored the basic blocks of TensorFlow.js to design, implement, and build a logistic regression and a linear regression model. These two models are examples of supervised learning, algorithms that use datasets made of features and labels to learn a function that maps these features to the labels.

For our next exercise, we will leave behind the topic of supervised learning and introduce its counterpart, **unsupervised learning**, and its quintessential algorithm, **k-means**.

Here, you will write a web app that trains a k-means model with an arbitrary dataset and visualize its different outcomes using the visualization library **Plotly**. Contrary to the previous two problems where you implemented the algorithms using the Layers API, in this one, you will use an external library named **ml5.js**. This library is a higher-level abstraction of TensorFlow.js that provides a simple interface to access several prebuilt and ready-to-use models. This exercise is inspired by the k-means example featured in the ml5.js GitHub page.[1]

---

[1]https://github.com/ml5js/ml5-examples/tree/development/d3/KMeans/ KMeans_GaussianClusterDemo

© Juan De Dios Santos Rivera 2020
J. Rivera, *Practical TensorFlow.js*, https://doi.org/10.1007/978-1-4842-6273-3_3

Understanding k-means

In a supervised learning setting, we are the teachers. Through the use of labels, we supervise the learning by telling the model "this is an apple," "this is spam," or "2000 steps equal 2 kilometers." But not in unsupervised learning—here, there are no labels or classes. Instead, since there is no outcome, the model's goal is to discover **associations** and **patterns** from the dataset's set of features.

The most canonical application of unsupervised learning is **clustering** (Murphy, 2013). This technique aims to partition a dataset into groups in such a way that similar data points are assigned to the same cluster while keeping those who are dissimilar in others. In a more mathematical language, this translates to minimizing the *intra-cluster distances* (also known as the pairwise dissimilarities) while maximizing the *inter-cluster distances* of the dissimilar points.

A prime example of a clustering algorithm is k-means, one that groups data observations by dividing an unlabeled dataset into *k* clusters. k-means works by iteratively moving the center of the *k* clusters to minimize the total inter-cluster distance (Gareth et al., 2013). The algorithm does this in one initial step and two iterative steps that run until convergence:

- The initial step, 0: Randomly select an initial set of *k* centers, known as centroids from among the data points.

- Assignment step, 1: Assign each data point to its nearest center using the Euclidean distance as the dissimilarity criteria.

- Update step, 2: For each centroid, calculate the mean of all points assigned to it. After that, the centroids move to the new mean value.

About ml5.js

The ml5.js library is a high-level interface of TensorFlow.js that enables us to quickly train algorithms like k-means and use pre-trained and ready-to-use models in just a few lines of code. According to its documentation, ml5.js aims to democratize the use of machine learning on the Web and make it approachable to a wide range of users, regardless of their technical background. Because of its simplicity and accessibility, ml5.js is a valuable tool for building prototypes.

Now you might ask: if it is so simple and friendly, why can't we use it all the time? Fair question. One answer is that being a high-level library blocks us from accessing all the vast functionalities and API that TensorFlow.js provides, which is, in my opinion, what makes it a rich framework.

About the data

This exercise features a synthetic dataset (it's the last one, I promise!). It has 100 observations, two features, and three classes that are not explicitly labeled, but that we will discover once we train the model. After all, that's the point of unsupervised learning.

Building the app

The application you will build here looks and feels similar to the ones you created in the previous chapter. Therefore, to avoid repeating and reading things we have already discussed, this tutorial will be more streamlined and less verbose than the last ones. This adjustment is also in part because we do not have to pre-process the data or define the model. Nonetheless, the methodology is still the same: download data, fit model, and visualize.

Setting up the workspace and the app's HTML

Let's start. As before, create a directory in your preferred location, and launch a web server using the tool *http-server*. To start the server, go to the terminal and execute http-server in the app's directory; by default, the server runs on port 8080. Next, go to the code editor and create the *index.html* file. In this file, you will design the app's interface and load the required libraries.

At the top of the file, add the necessary <html>, <head>, and <body> tags, and inside <head>, add two script tags to load ml5.js and Plotly. Note that we are not importing TensorFlow.js because ml5.js already does it:

```
<html>
<head>
  <!--Import ml5.js-->
  <script src="https://unpkg.com/ml5@0.4.3/dist/ml5.min.js"
  type="text/javascript"></script>
  <!--Import Plotly-->
  <script src='https://cdn.plot.ly/plotly-latest.min.js'>
  </script>
</head>
<body>
</body>
</html>
```

Inside the <body> element, create a <div>, and inside it, create an input of type *range*—<input type="range">—(not of type number, like we did before) and set its min and max attributes to 1 and 4, respectively, and the id to k-range. This element is a slider control for entering a number that is between the min and max values. You will use it to enter the desired number of clusters *k*. Then, below the input, add a <p> to display the input's value. The <div> should look like this:

```
<div>
  <h4>Enter K (1 to 4)</h4>
  <input type="range" id="k-range" min=1
   max="4" value="1">
  <p>k: <span id="k-value"></span></p>
</div>
```

Next, you have to implement a way to get the slider's value and update the paragraph's text so that it displays the selected k. To achieve this, we will use a script tag in the HTML to write JavaScript code. This script uses getElementById() to get the slider and paragraph and sets the paragraph's innerHTML property, aka the text, to the value assigned in the slider. However, this instruction runs only once. To make sure that the paragraph always shows the current k, you need an oninput event that executes a function every time the slider's value changes (something similar to the click listener from before). In this new function, you will change the paragraph's text to the slider's value:

```
<script>
    var slider = document
      .getElementById('k-range');
    var output = document
      .getElementById('k-value');
    output.innerHTML = slider.value;

    slider.oninput = function () {
        output.innerHTML = this.value;
    }
</script>
```

After closing the script tag, add an additional <div> with id set to button. Here, the program creates the button that starts the training.

Last, we need another <div> that will contain the Plotly visualization canvas (note that with tfjs-vis we didn't need any) and a script tag to start *index.js*. The complete *index.html* file should look like this:

```html
<html>
<head>
  <!--Import ml5.js-->
  <script src="https://unpkg.com/ml5@0.4.3/dist/ml5.min.js"
  type="text/javascript"></script>
  <!--Import Plotly-->
  <script src='https://cdn.plot.ly/plotly-latest.min.js'>
  </script>
</head>
<body>
    <div>
        <h4>Enter K (1 to 4)</h4>
        <input type="range" id="k-range" min="1"
         max="4" value="1">
        <p>k: <span id="k-value"></span></p>
    </div>

    <script>
        var slider = document
          .getElementById('k-range');
        var output = document
          .getElementById('k-value');
        output.innerHTML = slider.value;

        slider.oninput = function () {
            output.innerHTML = this.value;
        }
```

```
    </script>
    <div id="button"></div>
    <div id="plot"></div>
    <script src="./index.js"></script>
</body>
</html>
```

You may close *index.html* and create a new *index.js* file.

Training

The training function that fits an ml5.js k-means model is so simple and short that it makes the others look like the most complicated thing ever (well, they kind of are). It involves two statements. The first is an `options` object for configuring the model's number of clusters (`k`) and the max number of iterations (`maxIter`). Then, there's the call to the `kmeans` function.

The function's first parameter is the URL or local path to the dataset (see that we didn't even have to read the dataset manually?). The second one is the `options` object, and the third one a callback function that is called once the algorithm finishes. In the next segment of the tutorial, you will create a callback function that visualizes the clusters once the training ends. For now, let's simply write one that prints "Done." Also, note that the `options` object is an optional parameter. If none is used, the model uses the default values of `k=3` and `maxIter=5`.

In the following, you will find the complete training function, named `execute`, and the variables `model` and `csvUrl`. If you prefer using a local version of the dataset, you can find a copy in the repository:

```
let model;
```

```
const csvUrl = 'https://gist.githubusercontent.com/juandes/
34d4eb6dfd7217058d56d227eb077ca2/raw/c5c86ea7a32b5ae89ef06734
262fa8eff25ee776/cluster_df.csv';
```

```
async function execute(k) {
 // The k-means model configuration
 const options = {
   k,
   maxIter: 20,
 };

 // Arguments are: file's path, config, and a
 // callback that's called once the clustering ends
 model = ml5.kmeans(csvUrl, options, () => {
   console.log('Done :)');
 });
}
```

As we did earlier, we will implement a function named
createClusterButton() to create the button that initializes the training.
Once clicked, the button triggers an event that reads the slider's value and
uses it as an argument for execute():

```
function createClusterButton() {
  const btn = document.createElement('BUTTON');
  btn.innerText = 'Cluster!';

  btn.addEventListener('click', () => {
    const slider = document
      .getElementById('k-range');
    execute(slider.value);
  });

  document.querySelector('#button').appendChild(btn);
}
```

Last, create an init() function and call createClusterButton() from it. Afterward, call init():

```
function init() {
  createClusterButton();
}

init();
```

To run the system, start the local web server, and go to localhost:8080. There, you will see the slider, followed by its current value. Next, select the desired number of clusters *k* and click the "train" button. Nothing will happen or, well, at least nothing we can see (except the output from the callback function). In the next section, we'll turn this around and visualize the data along with the clustering outcome.

Visualizing the clusters

So far, we have been using tfjs-vis to visualize the datasets. But for this exercise's visualization, we will take a step away from tfjs-vis and introduce **Plotly**, a high-level JavaScript library for visualization, to plot the clustering.

The chart you will produce here is a scatter plot of the clustered dataset with each cluster represented with a predefined color and shape. The function that generates the plot, which we will call `visualizeResult()`, will be the model's callback function that is executed when the training ends. But before getting there, declare the following variables at the top of *index.js*:

```
const colMap = {
  0: 'black',
  1: 'green',
  2: 'blue',
  3: 'red',
};
```

85

```
const shapeMap = {
  0: 'circle',
  1: 'square',
  2: 'diamond',
  3: 'cross',
};
```

These maps are to differentiate the clusters on the plot. For example, the data points from cluster one are shown as black circles and those from cluster two as green squares. Next, we will do the function visualizeResult():

```
function visualizeResult() {
  const x = [];
  const y = [];
  const colors = [];
  const shapes = [];

  model.dataset.forEach((e) => {
    x.push(e[0]);
    y.push(e[1]);
    colors.push(colMap[e.centroid]);
    shapes.push(shapeMap[e.centroid]);
  });

  const trace = {
    x,
    y,
    mode: 'markers',
    type: 'scatter',
    marker: {
      symbol: shapes,
```

```
    color: colors,
  },
};

Plotly.newPlot('plot', [trace]);
}
```

To create a simple Plotly graph, you need to create *traces*, the term the library uses to refer to a collection of data. For this visualization, we have only one trace for drawing the clusters. At the beginning of the function, we iterate over model.dataset, an array of objects that contains the original dataset, plus an additional property named centroid, which indicates the data point's cluster. In each iteration, we push these values to different arrays while also mapping the cluster number to its respective color and shape. After the loop, define the trace and call Plotly.newPlot() with the argument 'plot' (the ID of the <div>) and the trace array.

That's the complete visualizeResult() function. Before closing the code editor and calling it a day, return to the kmeans() function, and replace the callback function with visualizeResult:

```
model = ml5.kmeans(csvUrl, options, visualizeResult);
```

Testing the model

Now it is time to test the model. So, head to the browser, run the app, and train. While at it, try all the different k's.

If k is 1 (Figure 3-1), you will notice that all the points have the same color and shape because they belong to the same cluster. In other words, according to the algorithm, every observation belongs to the same class.

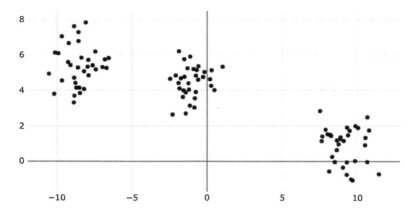

Figure 3-1. *Clustering using k=1. Note how all the data points are clustered under the same cluster*

However, we know this is not true because the dataset has three classes. Nevertheless, this trade-off between a small and large *k* is one of the main attributes of k-means. If chosen wrong, it might yield poor results. Yet, the flexibility of being able to control this value is also one of the key features, and we could also say advantages (or disadvantages, depending on your perspective) of the algorithm.

Regarding the other values of *k*, if it is 2, you will most likely have two blobs under the same cluster and the remaining one as another. If it equals 3, you might obtain a "perfect" cluster (what is perfect in unsupervised learning, anyway?) where each blob is its own cluster, and if *k* is 4, you will see one blob containing two classes (Figure 3-2).

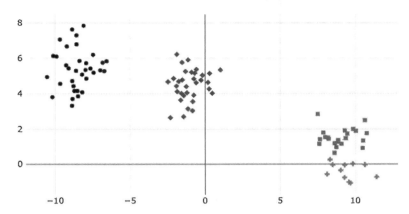

Figure 3-2. *Clustering using k=4. The data blob on the lower-right corner is split between two clusters*

Recap

In this exercise, we used the ml5.js library to fit a k-means. Compared to the previous examples, we saw how this library simplifies by order of magnitudes the procedure of creating and training a model. For example, we did not have to load the dataset, prepare the data, or define the model. Easy, right? However, as perfect as it seems, we need to understand that using such a library means losing some features that TensorFlow.js provides. Additional to the cluster, we introduced a visualization library, Plotly, to visualize them.

EXERCISES

---

1. What is unsupervised learning? How does it differ from supervised learning?

2. Name two cons and pros of ml5.js.

3. Add a slider or any input element to select the maximum number of iterations from the app.

4. Fit the model using the dataset from the logistic regression and check how the classes found by the algorithm differ from the real ones.

5. Implement the k-means algorithm from scratch. For some inspiration, refer to the ml5.js implementation found here: `https://github.com/ml5js/ml5-library/tree/development/src/KMeans.`

6. Add a third dimension to the dataset, cluster it, and visualize it with Plotly.

CHAPTER 4

Recognizing handwritten digits with convolutional neural networks

The models we trained in the past chapters offered us a glimpse of what we can do with TensorFlow.js. While insightful and useful, you could say that they were also uncomplicated. Those algorithms (linear regression, logistic regression, and k-means) were examples of traditional machine learning models. Typically, you would not use a tool like TF.js to implement them. Instead, most people would use a more specialized library like *scikit-learn*. Still, replicating them using a network-like structure is an excellent way to get started with TensorFlow's Layers API.

Now that we have a good understanding of the basics of the Layers API, we will move on from the simple networks and build our first complex one, a **convolutional neural network** (CNN). This class of model—which is probably the most popular deep learning algorithm—excels at extracting and recognizing visual features.

© Juan De Dios Santos Rivera 2020
J. Rivera, *Practical TensorFlow.js*, https://doi.org/10.1007/978-1-4842-6273-3_4

The application you will develop here is a handwritten digit detection app powered by a CNN trained on the **Modified National Institute of Standards and Technology (MNIST)** dataset. This web app features a canvas where the user will draw a digit that the model will identify in real-time.

Understanding convolutional neural networks

When we see a cat, we just know it is a cat. Right? We do not even think about it. But how does the brain do this? While the actual answer can span several books about neuroscience and the brain's visual cortex, for our purposes, we can summarize the explanation in one word: **features**. When you look at a kitty, you discern its features: the cute ears, whiskers, fluffy tail, and sharp claws—a cat.

A convolutional neural network (Y. LeCun et al., 1989) is a type of neural network that simulates the brain's visual cortex functions to extract and recognize the features of an image. Once extracted, the network learns that these features form the object, for example, a cat is a cat because of these features.

At its core, a CNN involves two layers: **convolutional** layer and **pooling** layer. The convolutional layer extracts the image's features. This layer has a convolutional kernel (often referred to as the **filter**), a tensor of size *height * width * depth*, that scan (the proper term is **convolve**) an input image (a tensor) starting from the top-left corner until it reaches the bottom-right.

At each convolution, the layer calculates the sum of the element-wise multiplication between the kernel and the area of the input it currently covers (known as the **receptive field**). The kernel's values, called the **weights**, are parameters adjusted by the learning algorithm. After sliding over the complete input, the result is a 2D array known as the **feature** (or activation) **map**, which is a reduced representation of the input's principal features. Note that a convolutional layer can have more than one filter. In such a case, the depth size is the number of filters.

Figure 4-1 presents an example of a convolution. At time t, the kernel of size 3x3 evaluates the top-left corner of the input and produces the value displayed on the feature map. Then, at $t + 1$ (Figure 4-2), the kernel slides one pixel to the right and repeats the process. By this point, since the kernel is at the rightmost part of the tensor, during the next step $t + 2$, it shifts down one unit and starts once again from the leftmost part of the input (cell [2,1]). The length of the slide (how many units it shifts) is called the **stride**. Figure 4-3 shows the last feature map.

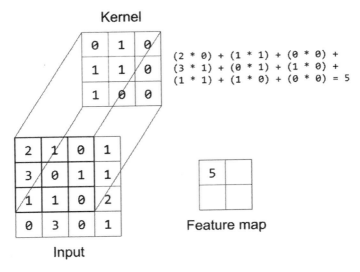

Figure 4-1. An example of a convolution with a kernel of size 3x3

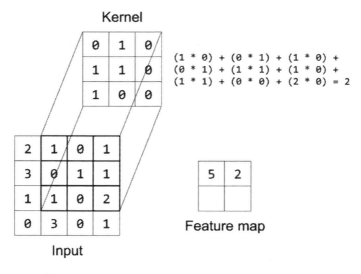

Figure 4-2. *The convolution at time t + 1*

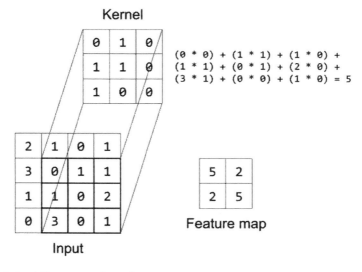

Figure 4-3. *The complete feature map*

Another attribute of the convolutional layer is the **padding**, a technique used to control the size of the layer's output by adding zero padding (a "border" of zeroes) to the input. That way, after the convolutions, the output's size remains the same as the input's size. Using padding allows the network to conserve the information at the edges of the image.

It is a common practice adding a **pooling layer** after a convolutional layer. These layers reduce (i.e., subsample) the spatial size of the input image to reduce the number of parameters of the network, lessening the risk of overfitting the model. As a direct consequence, having fewer parameters leads to a smaller model, decreasing the training time and the memory footprint.

Like a convolutional layer, a pooling layer involves a (pooling) kernel that scans the input. But instead of multiplying the receptive field by some weights (the pooling kernel has no weights), it aggregates and summarizes the receptive field's values using either a mean or max function. Figure 4-4 shows an example of a max pooling layer. In the image, you can see how each cell of the output is the max value of its receptive field.

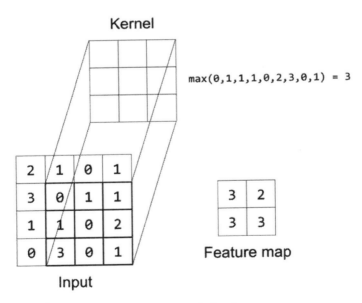

Figure 4-4. *A max pooling layer and the feature map*

95

Last, a convnet requires a fully connected layer (known as a dense layer in TF.js) to output the prediction.

To summarize, a convolutional neural network has two principal layers: convolutional and pooling. The first one extracts features from an image to learn how to identify it. For example, the network might know that a cat is a cat because it has sharp claws. After the convolution operation, the resulting tensor will have a smaller height and width (depending on the attributes used) and a depth that equals the number of filters used. The second layer, pooling, reduces the size of the input, resulting in a smaller and faster network. To visualize these concepts, Figure 4-5 presents the architecture of the CNN we will create, including the sizes of the inputs and the filters.

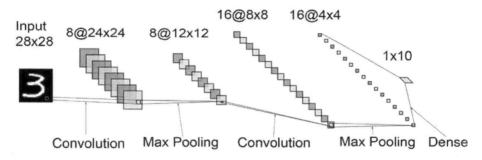

Figure 4-5. *A convolutional neural network*

About the MNIST dataset

The dataset we will use to train the convnet is the **Modified National Institute of Standards and Technology**, or MNIST (Yann LeCun et al., 2010), dataset of handwritten digits. This well-known dataset, often used for benchmarking machine learning models and architectures, has over 60,000 28x28 grayscale images of handwritten digits between 0 and 9. Figure 4-6 shows a sample.

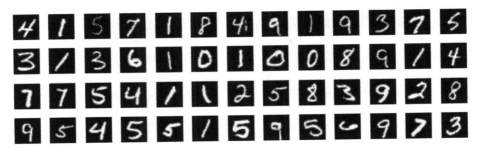

Figure 4-6. *Sample of MNIST digits*

Having more than two classes means that we will work in a **multiclass classification** problem, the task of classifying examples into one of three or more categories.

Building the app

For this chapter's exercise, you will make an app that fits a convolutional neural network using the MNIST dataset to identify handwritten digits in real-time. At first, as we did with the others, we will load the dataset, followed by designing the model and training it. Then, we will develop the drawing functionality, which involves setting up a canvas to draw the digit we wish to identify. After drawing the number, the app converts the image to a tensor and feeds it to the model to recognize the input value.

To start the exercise, create a new directory and start a local server in the same location.

The app's HTML file

In the directory, create the app's *index.html* file. At its top, after the `<html>` tag, create a `<head>` tag and import TF.js, tfjs-vis, and a CSS file named *style.css*. CSS, which stands for **Cascading Style Sheets**, is a language that describes the style of an HTML document. We will use it to change the appearance of several HTML elements:

```
<html>
<head>
    <script src="https://cdn.jsdelivr.net/npm/@tensorflow/tfjs">
    </script>
    <script src="https://cdn.jsdelivr.net/npm/@tensorflow/
    tfjs-vis"></script>
    <link href="./style.css" rel="stylesheet">
</head>
</html>
```

After `<head>,` create a new `<body>` tag, and inside it, add a `<div>` with id attribute `pipeline`. Inside this `<div>`, the app creates the buttons that load the data, compile and train the model, and clear the canvas:

```
<body>
    <h1>Handwritten Digits Detection App</h1>
    <div id="pipeline"></div>
</body>
```

After the `<div>` comes the `<canvas>`, an element for drawing graphics. Its id attribute is set to `draw-canvas` and the CSS class to `digits-canvas`. This style changes the canvas background color to black and centers it. After the canvas, add a `<p>` with id `predict-output` to present the model's inferred digit:

```
<canvas id="draw-canvas" class="digits-canvas"></canvas>
<p id="predict-output"></p>
```

98

Last, load the app's *index.js* JavaScript code and a second script named *data.js*. This file—obtained from the official TensorFlow.js examples repo—loads and prepares the MNIST dataset:

```
<script src="data.js" type="module"></script>
<script src="index.js" type="module"></script>
```

And that's it for the HTML. As for the CSS content, create a *style.css* file and add

```
.digits-canvas {
  background-color: black;
  display: block;
  margin: auto;
}
```

Loading and preparing the data

This exercise's MNIST dataset comes in one large sprite file. Because of this format, unraveling the data could get messy. To ease the task, we will use a script from the official TF.js examples repository that downloads, processes, and converts the data to a tensor.[1] But instead of just copying it and pasting it, let's go through it and understand what it does (then you can copy/paste without remorse). So, as the first step, create a new file and name it *data.js*.

---

[1]The original script is available at https://github.com/tensorflow/tfjs-examples/blob/master/mnist/data.js. It is released under the Apache License. You can find a copy at www.apache.org/licenses/LICENSE-2.0 and in the book's appendix.

The script starts with several variables related to the size of the images, the number of elements, and the URL of the dataset and the labels:

```
export const IMAGE_H = 28;
export const IMAGE_W = 28;
const IMAGE_SIZE = IMAGE_H * IMAGE_W;
const NUM_CLASSES = 10;
const NUM_DATASET_ELEMENTS = 65000;

const NUM_TRAIN_ELEMENTS = 55000;
const NUM_TEST_ELEMENTS = NUM_DATASET_ELEMENTS - NUM_TRAIN_
ELEMENTS;

const MNIST_IMAGES_SPRITE_PATH = 'https://storage.googleapis.
com/learnjs-data/model-builder/mnist_images.png';
const MNIST_LABELS_PATH = 'https://storage.googleapis.com/
learnjs-data/model-builder/mnist_labels_uint8';
```

Then comes the MnistData class, the object that loads and processes the data. This class involves five major components, a constructor, three methods, and one static function.

The constructor initializes two variables used to store the index of the last returned batch of data:

```
export class MnistData {
  constructor() {
    this.shuffledTrainIndex = 0;
    this.shuffledTestIndex = 0;
  }
}
```

After the constructor is the async method load(), responsible for loading the data. This method starts by reading the dataset from a remote location and assigning it to an instance of an Image object. Because the dataset is large, the next steps entail dividing it in chunks of *N* elements and adding them to an array:

```
async load() {
    const img = new Image();
    const canvas = document.createElement('canvas');
    const ctx = canvas.getContext('2d');
    const imgRequest = new Promise((resolve) => {
        img.crossOrigin = '';
        img.onload = () => {
            img.width = img.naturalWidth;
            img.height = img.naturalHeight;

            const datasetBytesBuffer = new ArrayBuffer(NUM_DATASET_
            ELEMENTS * IMAGE_SIZE * 4);

            const chunkSize = 5000;
            canvas.width = img.width;
            canvas.height = chunkSize;

            for (let i = 0; i < NUM_DATASET_ELEMENTS / chunkSize;
            i += 1) {
                const datasetBytesView = new Float32Array(
                    datasetBytesBuffer, i * IMAGE_SIZE * chunkSize * 4,
                    IMAGE_SIZE * chunkSize,
                );
                ctx.drawImage(
                    img, 0, i * chunkSize, img.width, chunkSize, 0, 0,
                    img.width,
                    chunkSize,
                );
```

```
    const imageData = ctx.getImageData(0, 0, canvas.width,
    canvas.height);

    for (let j = 0; j < imageData.data.length / 4;
    j += 1) {
      datasetBytesView[j] = imageData.data[j * 4] / 255;
    }
  }
  this.datasetImages = new Float32Array(datasetBytesBuffer);

  resolve();
};
img.src = MNIST_IMAGES_SPRITE_PATH;
});
```

After getting the image, the function fetches the dataset's labels and assigns it to another array. Once the arrays are ready, the last step is slicing them to split the data and labels into a training and test dataset:

```
const labelsRequest = fetch(MNIST_LABELS_PATH);
const [, labelsResponse] = await Promise.all([imgRequest,
labelsRequest]);

this.datasetLabels = new Uint8Array(await labelsResponse.
arrayBuffer());

this.trainIndices = tf.util.createShuffledIndices(NUM_TRAIN_
ELEMENTS);
this.testIndices = tf.util.createShuffledIndices(NUM_TEST_
ELEMENTS);
```

```
this.trainImages = this.datasetImages.slice(0, IMAGE_SIZE *
NUM_TRAIN_ELEMENTS);
this.testImages = this.datasetImages.slice(IMAGE_SIZE *
NUM_TRAIN_ELEMENTS);
this.trainLabels = this.datasetLabels.slice(0, NUM_CLASSES *
NUM_TRAIN_ELEMENTS);
this.testLabels = this.datasetLabels.slice(NUM_CLASSES *
NUM_TRAIN_ELEMENTS);
}
```

You may close the function.

Next is nextBatch(), a static function that returns a tensor containing a batch of data from the dataset. It has three parameters: batchSize, data, and index. batchSize refers to the size of the batch, data is the dataset, and index indicates from what index onward you want to get the batch:

```
static nextBatch(batchSize, data, index) {
    const batchImagesArray = new Float32Array(batchSize *
    IMAGE_SIZE);
    const batchLabelsArray = new Uint8Array(batchSize *
    NUM_CLASSES);

    for (let i = 0; i < batchSize; i += 1) {
      const idx = index();

      const image = data[0].slice(idx * IMAGE_SIZE, idx *
      IMAGE_SIZE + IMAGE_SIZE);
      batchImagesArray.set(image, i * IMAGE_SIZE);

      const label = data[1].slice(idx * NUM_CLASSES, idx *
      NUM_CLASSES + NUM_CLASSES);
      batchLabelsArray.set(label, i * NUM_CLASSES);
    }
```

```
  const xs = tf.tensor2d(batchImagesArray, [batchSize,
  IMAGE_SIZE]);
  const labels = tf.tensor2d(batchLabelsArray, [batchSize,
  NUM_CLASSES]);

  return { xs, labels };
}
```

As for the last functions, we have nextTrainBatch() and nextTestBatch(). They use nextBatch() to return the next batch of the train and test dataset, respectively:

```
nextTrainBatch(batchSize) {
    return MnistData.nextBatch(
      batchSize, [this.trainImages, this.trainLabels], () => {
        this.shuffledTrainIndex = (this.shuffledTrainIndex + 1)
        % this.trainIndices.length;
        return this.trainIndices[this.shuffledTrainIndex];
      },
    );
}

 nextTestBatch(batchSize) {
    return MnistData.nextBatch(batchSize, [this.testImages,
    this.testLabels], () => {
      this.shuffledTestIndex = (this.shuffledTestIndex + 1) %
      this.testIndices.length;
      return this.testIndices[this.shuffledTestIndex];
    });
}
```

To summarize, this file has a class `MnistData` that loads the data from a remote location and returns it in batches. A copy of the dataset is available in the book's repository.

Defining the network

Because the model we are about to create is significantly larger than the past ones, we will split the designing and the training part into two sections and, thus, in two individual functions. In this part, we will focus only on defining the architecture.

This app's convolutional neural network has seven layers (Figure 4-7)—a big jump when compared to the earlier models made up of one layer. The model's first layer is a convolutional layer named `tf.layers.conv2d` in TensorFlow.js. As we saw earlier, it is common to use a max pooling layer after a convolution, and so the second layer is a max pooling or `tf.layers.maxPooling2d`. This combination of convolutional and max pooling repeats once, making up layers 3 and 4. At the end of the network, we have a dropout layer (`tf.layers.dropout`), a flatten layer (`tf.layers.flatten`), and a dense layer. We will get to know them better as we design the network.

```
Layer (type)                    Output shape          Param #
=================================================================
conv2d_Conv2D1 (Conv2D)         [null,24,24,8]          208

max_pooling2d_MaxPooling2D1     [null,12,12,8]           0

conv2d_Conv2D2 (Conv2D)         [null,8,8,16]          3216

max_pooling2d_MaxPooling2D2     [null,4,4,16]            0

dropout_Dropout1 (Dropout)      [null,4,4,16]            0

flatten_Flatten1 (Flatten)      [null,256]               0

dense_Dense1 (Dense)            [null,10]             2570
=================================================================
Total params: 5994
Trainable params: 5994
Non-trainable params: 0
```

Figure 4-7. *The model's layers*

In the project's directory, create a file and name it *index.js*. In the file, declare the variables model, data, and isModelTrained and two constant ones that define the size of each data sample and depth. The first of these, IMAGE_SIZE, equals 28 because an MNIST digit's size is 28x28, while the second one, IMAGE_CHANNELS, is 1 because the images are grayscale.

```
let model;
let data;
let isModelTrained = false;
const IMAGE_SIZE = 28;
const IMAGE_CHANNELS = 1;
```

Next write a new function, defineModel(). Inside it, create an instance of tf.Sequential and assign it to model. Then, append the first convolutional layer:

```
function defineModel() {
 model = tf.sequential();
 model.add(tf.layers.conv2d({
   inputShape: [IMAGE_SIZE, IMAGE_SIZE, IMAGE_CHANNELS],
   kernelSize: [5, 5],
   filters: 8,
   strides: 1,
   activation: 'relu',
 }));
}
```

Let's describe what's happening here. The attribute inputShape specifies the shape of the input values, that is, 28x28x1. Below it is the kernelSize, the dimensionality of the convolutional kernel; for this model, we will use a window of [5,5]. Then comes the number of filters (8) we will apply to the input. The next hyperparameter, stride, has a value of 1, meaning that the kernel moves one pixel at a time. Last, we have the activation function, which, in this case, is ReLU, short for a **rectified linear unit**. After the convolutions, the output of this layer is of shape [24, 24, 8] (see how the length and width decrease while the depth increases?) As a side note, it is worth mentioning that the layer's name is conv2d because the kernel convolves along two spatial dimensions (x and y).

Note   ReLU is a popular activation function used in convolutional neural networks (LeCun et al., 2015). A ReLU layer applies the element-wise function $max(0, x)$ to the input tensor, introducing nonlinearity to the network. The result is a tensor whose values are greater than 0, or 0.

The second layer you will add is a max pooling layer of filter size [2,2] and stride 2. After the pooling operation, the output tensor is of shape [12, 12, 8]:

```
model.add(tf.layers.maxPooling2d({
    poolSize: [2, 2],
    strides: 2,
}));
```

Next comes a second convolutional layer. Its attributes are the same as the last one, except for the number of filters (16) and the lack of input shape, which you do not have to specify because it is not the network's first layer. This layer produces a tensor of shape [8, 8, 16]:

```
model.add(tf.layers.conv2d({
    kernelSize: [5, 5],
    filters: 16,
    strides: 1,
    activation: 'relu',
}));
```

You will also need another max pooling layer. After this one, the output's shape is [4, 4, 16] (see how it shrinks?):

```
model.add(tf.layers.maxPooling2d({
    poolSize: [2, 2],
    strides: 2,
}));
```

Now let's introduce the **dropout** layer. Dropout (Srivastava et al., 2014) is a very popular regularization technique that helps to prevent overfitting. This operation forces a network to drop out and ignore a random fraction of input units during the current training step. Dropping units causes the network to "reevaluate" how it will train during the current iteration, which means trying to obtain a low loss value while using fewer parts of the network. In simple words, dropouts prevent the network from getting too comfortable. On this occasion, use a dropout layer with a "dropping" rate of 0.3, meaning that the training will not use 30% of the units. The shape of the output remains unchanged:

```
model.add(tf.layers.dropout({ rate: 0.3 }));
```

After the dropout, add a **flatten** layer. This layer flattens the input into a 1D tensor of shape [256]. This tensor is the feature vector that the last layer uses to produce the classification:

```
model.add(tf.layers.flatten());
```

To conclude the model, we need a fully connected layer or dense in TensorFlow speech. This layer produces the network's output, which, in this case, is the predicted digit. Our goal here is to produce a vector of length 10 (one for each digit) where each value is the probability for each class. To achieve this, we need to set the units attribute (the dimensionality of the output space) to 10 and use a **softmax** activation function. This function converts the raw and non-normalized predictions (known as **logits**) to actual probabilities:

```
model.add(tf.layers.dense({
    units: 10,
    activation: 'softmax',
}));
```

Phew! Those were a lot of layers. To make sure we got everything right, let's recap what we just did. The network has seven layers. The first four—two convolutional and two max pooling—extract the features of the image and reduce its size. After them is a dropout layer that ignores 30% of the units on each training iteration. For the output, we used a flatten layer to flat the tensor and a dense layer with a softmax activation function to produce a vector with the probabilities of the predictions.

As for the very last step, compile the model to prepare it for the training. On this occasion, we will once again use the Adam optimizer and accuracy metric. As for the loss function, the proper one for this case is **categorical cross-entropy** (CCE). Like the binary cross-entropy (BCE) function from Chapter 2, this one also measures how far a prediction is from its real value and then averages the errors to obtain the loss value. The distinction between them is that CCE is for multiclass classification problems, while BCE suits binary classification situations:

```
model.compile({
    optimizer: tf.train.adam(),
    loss: 'categoricalCrossentropy',
    metrics: ['accuracy'],
});
```

You could use `model.summary()` after compiling the model to print a table of the layers and their output sizes.

With this, we conclude the model (and this function). Before moving on, we need to understand that the perfect architecture does not exist. Sure, there are common practices, rules of thumb, and even architectures with proper names, for example, *LeNet-5* (Yann LeCun et al., 1998), *AlexNet* (Krizhevsky et al., 2012), and the humongous *ResNet* (He et al., 2015) with 152 layers. But in general, you need to find a configuration that suits the data. I know it is easier said than done, but with practice, I promise you will get better. The architecture we just designed is a standard one you will find in the literature for the MNIST dataset. Yet, for illustration and teaching purposes, I changed it by adding the dropout layer.

Training the model

With the model compiled, let's get into the fun part: the training. Even though the model's design differs from the ones we have already created, training it follows the same procedure as the others: load data and fit.

Start by creating a new function, train(), and the variables BATCH_SIZE, TRAIN_DATA_SIZE, and TEST_DATA_SIZE:

```
const BATCH_SIZE = 512;
const TRAIN_DATA_SIZE = 6000;
const TEST_DATA_SIZE = 1000;

async function train() {

}
```

After the variables, go to the very start of the file and add the following line to import the MnistData class from *data.js*:

```
import { MnistData } from './data.js';
```

Back in the function train(), add the following:

```
const [xTrain, yTrain] = tf.tidy(() => {
   const d = data.nextTrainBatch(TRAIN_DATA_SIZE);
   return [
     d.xs.reshape([TRAIN_DATA_SIZE, IMAGE_SIZE, IMAGE_SIZE, 1]),
     d.labels,
   ];
});
```

In this statement, we are using tf.tidy() to assign to xTrain and yTrain a part of the training set (and its labels) using nextTrainBatch(). tf.tidy() is a function that takes as argument a function fn and cleans up the tensors allocated by fn once fn finishes its execution (the tensors returned by fn are not cleaned).

We are explicitly managing the memory because in the WebGL backend mode, the tensors are not automatically garbage collected. But do not worry! In this example, memory is not an issue. Nonetheless, it is good to acknowledge this limitation and the `tf.tidy()` function. If you are curious about the app's memory allocation, use `tf.memory()` to get a summary of the memory usage.

Note   Use `tensor.dispose()` to dispose any tensor and release its memory.

Use the same approach to load the test dataset. Later, you will use this data to test the model's predictive capability with cases it did not encounter during the training phase:

```
const [xTest, yTest] = tf.tidy(() => {
   const d = data.nextTestBatch(TEST_DATA_SIZE);
   return [
      d.xs.reshape([TEST_DATA_SIZE, IMAGE_SIZE, IMAGE_SIZE, 1]),
      d.labels,
   ];
});
```

Now, we fit the model. Unlike the previous cases, we will train using `tf.Sequential.fit()`, instead of the `tf.Sequential.fitDataset()` function because this time, the dataset is not a `tf.data.Dataset` object. Besides this minor detail, both functions are the same:

```
await model.fit(xTrain, yTrain, {
   batchSize: BATCH_SIZE,
   epochs: 30,
   validationData: [xTest, yTest],
```

```
    shuffle: true,
    callbacks: tfvis.show.fitCallbacks(
      { name: 'Loss and Accuracy', tab: 'Training' },
      ['loss', 'val_loss', 'acc', 'val_acc'],
    ),
  });
```

```
  isModelTrained = true;
```

model.fit() has three arguments: the training data, the labels, and a ModelFitConfig object that specifies the model's hyperparameters and other attributes. The first of these hyperparameters is batchSize, and we will set it to BATCH_SIZE (512). This number defines the number of data samples the model examines before updating its weights.[2] Before, we did not explicitly set this number and used its default value, 32. Then, set epochs to 30.

After the hyperparameters, use the attribute validationData to set the validation dataset and labels. During training, the model uses the validation dataset to evaluate its performance, producing an extra set of loss (validation loss) and metrics (validation accuracy) at the end of each epoch. This dataset is not part of the training data. As the name points out, the validation data is to evaluate the model with data it did not see during training.

Next, set shuffle to true to shuffle the training data before each epoch, and use tfvis.show.fitCallbacks() to create the visualization callbacks. This time, the app will generate graphs of the loss and accuracy metric for both training and validation data after each batch and epoch. Before closing the function, change isModelTrained to true.

---

[2]If the dataset's length is not a multiple of BATCH_SIZE, the final batch will have fewer samples than the others.

Creating the drawing canvas

The last component needed before completing the app is the drawing mechanism. To draw the numbers, you will use the canvas element defined in the HTML and four different event listeners.

To begin with, at the top of the file (beneath the const variables), add the following new variables:

```
let lastPosition = { x: 0, y: 0 };
let drawing = false;
let ctx;
const canvasSize = 200;
```

Now, create a new function and call it prepareCanvas(). In the first lines of the function, get the canvas and its context using getElementById(). The context object provides the properties and methods needed to draw and modify the canvas. Through the context, change the strokeStyle, fillStyle, lineJoin (the shape of the corner that joins two lines), lineCap (the shape of the endpoints), and lineWidth:

```
function prepareCanvas() {
 const canvas = document.getElementById('draw-canvas');
 canvas.width = canvasSize;
 canvas.height = canvasSize;
 ctx = canvas.getContext('2d');
 ctx.strokeStyle = 'white';
 ctx.fillStyle = 'white';
 ctx.lineJoin = 'round';
 ctx.lineCap = 'round';
 ctx.lineWidth = 15;
}
```

Next, create the first of the canvas event listeners. This one, of type mousedown, sets `drawing` to `true` and gets the offsets of the mouse. The event triggers when the user holds down the mouse button while inside the canvas. Conversely, add a mouseout event to change the variable drawing to `false` when the user moves the cursor out of the canvas:

```
canvas.addEventListener('mousedown', (e) => {
    drawing = true;
    lastPosition = { x: e.offsetX, y: e.offsetY };
});

canvas.addEventListener('mouseout', () => {
    drawing = false;
});
```

Then comes the mousemove event, triggered when the user moves the mouse within the canvas. The event's first line checks if `drawing` is `true`. If not, then return; otherwise, draw. The drawing procedure involves using `moveTo` to set the starting point of the line, `lineTo` to specify where you want to draw the line, and `stroke` to outline the line:

```
canvas.addEventListener('mousemove', (e) => {
    if (!drawing) {
        return;
    }

    ctx.beginPath();
    ctx.moveTo(lastPosition.x, lastPosition.y);
    ctx.lineTo(e.offsetX, e.offsetY);
    ctx.stroke();
    lastPosition = { x: e.offsetX, y: e.offsetY };
});
```

The last event needed, mouseup, fires up when the user removes the mouse from the canvas. When this happens, the function reads the canvas' image, converts it to a tensor, and predicts. Converting the image to a tensor requires using several methods to ensure that it has the right shape and format. These steps are

1. resizeBilinear(): Resizes the tensor to 28x28.

2. mean(): Converts the images to grayscale.

3. expandDims(): Reshapes the tensor to [1, 28, 28, 1].

4. float(): Casts the values to floats.

5. div(): Divides the values by 255 to normalize them between 0 and 1. Why 255? Because a grayscale image's values are in the [0, 255] range.

With the processed tensor, use model.predict() to predict and tf.Tensor.dataSync() to retrieve the values of the resulting tensor. Then, use tf.argMax() to return the index of the prediction's vector maximum value—remember that softmax produces a vector of probabilities where the largest number corresponds to the predicted class, for example, in vector [0, 0.10, 0.999, 0.093, 0.891, 0.673, 0.453, 0.381, 0.449, 0.300], the largest value is on index 2, so the predicted class is the digit "2." To present the prediction in the app, use the <p> with id predict-output and the innerHTML attribute:

```
canvas.addEventListener('mouseup', () => {
    drawing = false;

    if (!isModelTrained) {
        return;
    }
```

```
   const toPredict = tf.browser.fromPixels(canvas)
     .resizeBilinear([IMAGE_SIZE, IMAGE_SIZE])
     .mean(2)
     .expandDims()
     .expandDims(3)
     .toFloat()
     .div(255.0);

   const prediction = model.predict(toPredict).dataSync();

   const p = document
     .getElementById('predict-output');
   p.innerHTML = `Predicted value is: ${tf.argMax(prediction).
   dataSync()}`;
});
```

Putting it all together

Almost there! By this point, we have yet created none of the app's buttons, and since the app needs several, we will use a function to produce them. That way, we can avoid repeating the same code. The following is the function:

```
function createButton(innerText, selector, id, listener,
disabled = false) {
 const btn = document.createElement('BUTTON');
 btn.innerText = innerText;
 btn.id = id;
 btn.disabled = disabled;

 btn.addEventListener('click', listener);

 document.querySelector(selector).appendChild(btn);
}
```

createButton() has five parameters, including an optional one. The first, innerText, assigns the button's text. Following it is selector used here to select the <div> where you want to insert the button. The rest are the button's id, the event listener, and a flag to disable the button.

You will also need drawData(), a function that visualizes a sample of the dataset in the tfjs-vis visor. Unlike the earlier visualizations, this one does not use any prebuilt charts (like the scatter plot). Instead, we will add the sample images to a canvas and display the canvas in the visor (yes, that is possible!):

```
const dataSurface = { name: 'Sample', tab: 'Data' };

async function drawData() {
 const surface = tfvis.visor().surface(dataSurface);
 const numSamples = 20;
 let digit;

 const sample = data.nextTestBatch(numSamples);

 for (let i = 0; i < numSamples; i += 1) {
   digit = tf.tidy(() => sample.xs
     .slice([i, 0], [1, sample.xs.shape[1]])
     .reshape([IMAGE_SIZE, IMAGE_SIZE, 1]));

   const visCanvas = document.createElement('canvas');
   visCanvas.width = IMAGE_SIZE;
   visCanvas.height = IMAGE_SIZE;
   visCanvas.style = 'margin: 5px;';
   await tf.browser.toPixels(digit, visCanvas);
   surface.drawArea.appendChild(visCanvas);
 }
}
```

Note   ESLint disapproves await in loops, but in this case, we can safely ignore the rule.

If you wish, you can move dataSurface to the top of the file.

To conclude the app, create the following init() function and the helper enableButtons(), used to enable the buttons at a particular stage of the app's life cycle:

```
function enableButton(selector) {
  document.getElementById(selector).disabled = false;
}
function init() {
  prepareCanvas();
  createButton('Load data', '#pipeline', 'load-btn',
    async () => {
      data = new MnistData();
      await data.load();
      drawData();
      enableButton('train-btn');
    });

  createButton('Train', '#pipeline', 'train-btn',
    async () => {
      defineModel();
      train();
    }, true);

  createButton('Clear', '#pipeline', 'clear-btn',
    () => {
      ctx.clearRect(0, 0, canvasSize, canvasSize);
    });
}

init();
```

119

The function uses `prepareCanvas()` and `createButton()` to construct three buttons. The first button loads and draws a sample of the data. Button number two (disabled by default) compiles and trains the model, and the third one resets the drawing canvas.

Pat yourself in the back. You finished! Now, let's see the app in action.

Trying the app

To test the app, return to the terminal and start the local web server using *http-server*. Then click the address shown to access the application. There, you should see the three buttons and the canvas below them. Now click the "load" button to load and visualize the data. It should take a few seconds to download the dataset. Once downloaded, the tfjs-vis visor will open and display a sample of the dataset like the one in Figure 4-6.

By this point, the "train" button should be functional again—click it to compile and train the model. If you added the call to `model.summary()` in `defineModel()`, open the browser's developer console to see the model's summary, which includes the layers and output shapes.

Since we have a deeper model and a larger dataset than those from Chapters 2 and 3, the training time is significantly longer. Instead of taking a few seconds, this one could extend up to 5 minutes. So, while it trains, take a small break and get a glass of water.

If you look at the visor, you will find the `onBatchEnd` and `onEpochEnd` charts. From them, we can conclude that it took around 100 batches or 8 epochs to achieve a reasonable accuracy greater than 80%. The final accuracy is around 95% for both the training and validation set (Figure 4-8).

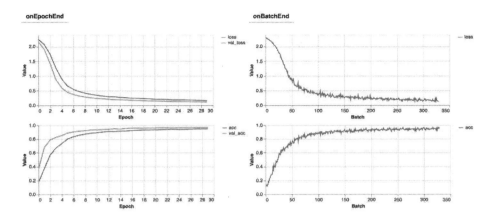

Figure 4-8. *The model's metrics*

Once the training ends, the canvas is all yours to draw digits. Below it, you will see the model's prediction. To clear the canvas, click the "clear" button. Figure 4-9 presents a screenshot.

Handwritten Digits Detection App

Figure 4-9. *A drawn 8 and the model's response*

Recap and conclusion

Convolutional neural networks have become a staple of deep learning and artificial intelligence. Ever since their return in the early 2010s, this architecture has become the principal component of numerous apps, systems, and platforms we have heard of, encounter, and even use in our daily lives. For example, CNNs are the engine that powers up self-driving cars, facial recognition software, and object detection systems (we will build one later!), among others. Although visual applications are their major target, it is not rare using convnets for other tasks, that is, speech recognition (Abdel-Hamid et al., 2014).

In this chapter, we built an app that uses a convolutional neural network trained on the MNIST dataset to recognize handwritten digits. At its core, the model consists of two convolutional layers, two max pooling layers, and a fully connected layer that produces the result. After training it on 30 epochs, the model achieved an accuracy of around 95%. As impressive as it sounds, we should know our score is very far from some of the highest scores reached, for example, 99.80% (Wan et al., 2013). But do not let this discourage you! As part of the exercises, I would invite you to revisit the model and improve the score. And who knows, maybe I see your paper sometime in the future.

EXERCISES

1. Modify the network to improve the error rate.

2. Fit a non-convolutional neural network with the dataset.

3. Implement a convolutional neural network architecture found in the literature, for example, AlexNet.

4. What are stride and kernel size? How do they affect the tensor's output shape?

5. What is the difference between a convolutional and a pooling layer?

6. Check out the paper "Backpropagation applied to handwritten zip code recognition" (Y. LeCun et al., 1989) to see one of the first mentions of a convolutional neural network.

CHAPTER 5

Making a game with PoseNet, a pose estimator model

Time for a fun application! Are you ready to pose? I hope so, because in this exercise your movements are the test dataset.

In this chapter, you will implement a game that features the model known as **PoseNet**. PoseNet is a neural network capable of doing real-time human pose estimation in images and videos. In this context, estimating a pose refers to the task of identifying where a person's body joints and other parts appear in a frame. For example, Figure 5-1 is a screenshot from the app, and on the canvas located at the center, you can see a skeleton overlay showing the parts of the body identified by the algorithm.

With PoseNet, we will introduce the book's first pre-trained and built-in model. So, since we do not have to train it, our work reduces to understanding the algorithm's output and building the game around it.

The application you will create is a game where the user has to show to PoseNet, through the device's webcam, a series of body parts before time runs out. If PoseNet identifies the part, the user gets one point. Otherwise, it gets a strike.

© Juan De Dios Santos Rivera 2020
J. Rivera, *Practical TensorFlow.js*, https://doi.org/10.1007/978-1-4842-6273-3_5

Figure 5-1. *A screenshot of the game. I'm not very good at it*

What is PoseNet?

PoseNet is a convolutional neural network model for estimating human poses. These poses are made from a group of 17 different and predefined body parts, known as **keypoints**. These are both eyes, ears, shoulders, elbows, wrists, hips, knees, ankles, and the nose.

The model has two methods of decoding the poses: *single-person pose estimator* and *multiple-person pose estimator*. The single pose estimator is faster and requires fewer resources. But its disadvantage is that if multiple subjects are present in the frame, the model might estimate the pose from all of them. For example, in the case of having two people in the video, the algorithm might detect the left eye from subject A and the right eye from subject B. The multiple poses estimator handles this problem. This method can recognize if the poses come from different bodies, at the cost of being slower than the single pose estimator (Oved, 2018). For this game, we will use the single pose detector.

Estimating a pose with PoseNet involves two key steps: computing **heatmaps** and **offset vectors**. The heatmaps are three-dimensional tensors of size RESOLUTION x RESOLUTION x 17 (the algorithm automatically squares the image), where the number 17 represents the keypoints. Each of the heatmaps' values is the confidence or probability that the corresponding keypoint is present at that location. Figure 5-2 presents a simplified example of the "right knee" keypoint heatmap.

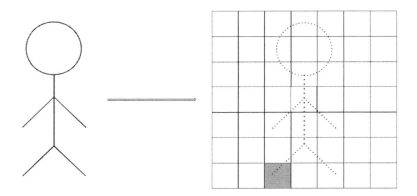

Figure 5-2. *A "right knee" heatmap*

In the second step, PoseNet calculates a set of offset vectors that measure the distance between the pixel and the keypoint location, producing, and I quote one of the papers behind the model, "a more precise estimating of the corresponding keypoint location" (Papandreou et al., 2017). After creating these tensors, the network aggregates them to produce highly localized activation maps that pinpoint the position of the keypoints (Figure 5-3).

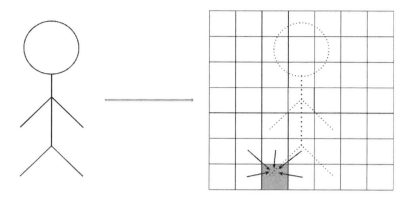

Figure 5-3. *The "right knee" offset vectors*

PoseNet comes in two flavors: the **MobileNet** and **ResNet** variants. The one we will use is the MobileNet-based variant. MobileNet (Howard et al., 2017) is a CNN architecture that sacrifices accuracy in favor of speed and size, making it ideal for a time-sensitive use case like a game. We will revisit and learn more about MobileNet in Chapter 8. The second variation is based on ResNet (He et al., 2015), a more accurate albeit slower and larger architecture.

The COCO dataset

The PoseNet model was trained on the **Common Objects in Context** or COCO keypoints (Lin et al., 2014) dataset. This dataset, created for the COCO Keypoint Detection Task competition, has more than 200,000 images with over 250,000 instances of people performing everyday tasks in uncontrolled conditions.

Building the game

The game you are about to create is a movement game where the user has to perform the pose presented on screen. For example, if the game says "leftHip," display your left hip on the webcam (please be careful). But you have to be fast and strike the pose in the allocated time. Otherwise, you will get a strike, and like every classic video game, you only have three. On the other hand, if you are doing great and dominating those poses like a dancer, the game gets harder. And harder means having less time to pose and triggering the "inverse" mode, a game mode where the user gets a strike if the prompted keypoint is present in the frame. So, if you see "~nose" on the screen, hide the nose from the camera.

Since we are using a pre-trained model and making a game, this exercise will differ from the others. You will start by setting up the camera, followed by loading and integrating the model and writing the gameplay loop. Unlike the earlier examples, there's no data pre-processing, training, and visualization tasks involved.

Structuring the UI

The game UI is very simple (Figure 5-1). It has a canvas presenting the webcam video with the keypoints and "skeleton" placed on top of the feed. Above the video is a button to start the game and another one to stop it. Under them are the game's score and strikes. On the sides of the canvas are the keypoint to pose and the timer. At the bottom is a label that notifies if the pose is correct or wrong.

Now to code it. As usual, create a new directory in your location of choice, and start a web server at the same place. Next, open the code editor and create a file named *index.html* and *style.css*. At the top of the file, use a <head> tag to import TensorFlow.js, PoseNet, and the CSS file:

```
<html>
<head>
  <script src="https://cdn.jsdelivr.net/npm/@tensorflow/tfjs">
  </script>
  <script src="https://cdn.jsdelivr.net/npm/@tensorflow-models/
  posenet"></script>
  <link href="./style.css" rel="stylesheet">
</head>
</html>
```

After <head>, add the <body> tag. Inside this node, write a title for the app and a <div> with id attribute game-container for the game UI. As stated earlier, the game UI has a set of buttons that you will create programmatically inside a <div> with id attribute buttons-menu. Below it, define another <div> used to display the game's score and strikes:

```
<body>
 <h2 class="center">Pose for the Net!</h2>
 <div class="game-container">
   <div id="buttons-menu" class="center" style="margin-top:
   25px;"></div>
   <div id="menu" class="game-ui">
     <div class="center">
       <p>Score:</p>
       <p id="score">0</p>
     </div>
```

```
  <div class="center">
    <p>Strikes:</p>
    <p id="strikes">0</p>
  </div>
</div>
</body>
```

Under the last <div>, create another one. This one has the "pose to match" string, the timer, the <video> tag used to retrieve the webcam feed, and the canvas that displays the video and the keypoints:

```
<div class="game-ui">
  <div class="center">
    <p id='pose-to-match' style="font-size:80px;">-</p>
  </div>
  <div>
    <video id="video" playsinline style="display: none;">
    </video>
    <canvas id="output"></canvas>
  </div>
  <div class="center">
    <p id="countdown" style="font-size:80px;">-</p>
  </div>
</div>
<div id="result" class="center">
  <p id="result-text" style="font-size: 60px;"></p>
</div>
</div>
```

After the <div>, add two <scripts> to load *index.js* and *draw.js*, a script with functions that draw the keypoints and skeleton over the canvas. The *draw.js* script (which I slightly changed) comes from the PoseNet example in the official TensorFlow.js repository:[1]

```
<script src="draw.js" type="module"></script>
<script src="index.js" type="module"></script>
```

To end this section, copy the following CSS code (for centering and positioning the elements) in *style.css*:

```
.center {
  margin: auto;
  width: 50%;
  display: flex;
  justify-content: center;
}

.game-container {
  margin: auto;
}

.game-container h2 {
  font-size: 15px;
  padding: 10px;
  color: white;
  border-top-left-radius: 5px;
  border-top-right-radius: 5px;
}
```

---

[1]https://github.com/tensorflow/tfjs-models/blob/master/posenet/demos/
 demo_util.js

```css
.game-ui {
  display: flex;
  flex-wrap: wrap;
}

.game-ui div {
  flex: 1;
  padding: 20px;
  text-align: center;
}
```

Setting up the camera

Create the *index.js* file. On the first line, add the variable SIZE (the size of the canvas width and height) and set its value to 500. Following this, create the new function setupCamera():

```javascript
const SIZE = 500;
function setupCamera() {
  const video = document.getElementById('video');
  video.width = SIZE;
  video.height = SIZE;

  navigator.mediaDevices.getUserMedia({
    audio: false,
    video: {
      width: SIZE,
      height: SIZE,
    },
  }).then((stream) => {
    video.srcObject = stream;
  });
```

```
  return new Promise((resolve) => {
    video.onloadedmetadata = () => resolve(video);
  });
}
```

The first lines of setupCamera() get the video element and set its size. It uses MediaDevices.getUserMedia()[2] to produce a Promise whose intended value is a MediaStream (the video). We will get the value using a then statement. In it, use a callback to set the webcam stream to the video element. This method triggers the pop-up that requests permission to access the video (accept!).

There is a second function you will need, loadVideo(). The function calls setupCamera() and uses its method play() to play the video:

```
async function loadVideo() {
 const video = await setupCamera();
 video.play();

 return video;
}
```

Now, let's draw and present the video on the canvas. So, create a new function, detect(), that takes the video as an argument. In the function, get the canvas element and its context and set the size. Within the function, add a second one (yes, inside), and name it getPose(). Later, you will add here the code responsible for performing the predictions. For now, let's focus on drawing the video on the canvas.

---

[2]https://developer.mozilla.org/en-US/docs/Web/API/MediaDevices/
 getUserMedia

Instead of drawing the video feed as it is, we will use ctx.scale() and ctx.translate() to flip it, so it looks more natural to us. After preparing the context, use requestAnimationFrame(), a JavaScript function that, in this circumstance, is used to produce the next frame of the video. Now, close getPose(), and call it from the next line (while still in detect()).

```
function detect(video) {
 const canvas = document.getElementById('output');
 const ctx = canvas.getContext('2d');
 canvas.width = SIZE;
 canvas.height = SIZE;

 async function getPose() {
   ctx.clearRect(0, 0, SIZE, SIZE);

   ctx.save();
   ctx.scale(-1, 1);
   ctx.translate(-SIZE, 0);
   ctx.drawImage(video, 0, 0, SIZE, SIZE);
   ctx.restore();
   requestAnimationFrame(getPose);
 }

 getPose();
}
```

Before moving on to the exciting part of the game, take a small pause to check that everything is running as expected. So, create an init() function, and call loadVideo(), and detect() from it. Next, call init():

```
async function init() {
 const video = await loadVideo();
 detect(video);
}

init();
```

With the web server running, go to the browser and start the app. Right away, a pop-up shows up, asking for permission to access the camera. After accepting, the webcam feed will appear in the middle of the app.

Loading and testing the model

The app is running, and you can see yourself on the canvas. Good. So, as the next step, you will load the model and do a quick test to check out how it works and to understand better the prediction object it returns.

Back at the code editor, create a new file and name it *draw.js*. This file hosts the functions that draw the PoseNet keypoints and the skeleton on the canvas. Before getting to the functions, declare a variable COLOR and set it to "red" (or any other color) to paint every line and dot with red. Then create a function that draws the points; call it drawPoint():

```
const COLOR = 'red';

function drawPoint(ctx, y, x, r) {
 ctx.beginPath();
 ctx.arc(x, y, r, 0, 2 * Math.PI);
 ctx.fillStyle = COLOR;
 ctx.fill();
}
```

You might realize that some context methods are those we saw in Chapter 5. The only exception is ctx.arc(), one that draws circles.

After drawPoint(), create drawSegment(), a function that draws the lines between keypoints:

```
function drawSegment([ay, ax], [by, bx], scale, ctx) {
 ctx.beginPath();
 ctx.moveTo(ax * scale, ay * scale);
 ctx.lineTo(bx * scale, by * scale);
```

```
ctx.lineWidth = '10px';
ctx.strokeStyle = COLOR;
ctx.stroke();
}
```

Next comes drawSkeleton() alongside its helper function toTuple(). drawSkeleton() uses PoseNet's getAdjacentKeyPoints() method to get the points near the keypoints and drawSegment() to draw the lines:

```
function toTuple({ y, x }) {
 return [y, x];
}
```

```
export function drawSkeleton(keypoints, minConfidence, ctx,
scale = 1) {
 const adjacentKeyPoints = posenet.
getAdjacentKeyPoints(keypoints, minConfidence);

 adjacentKeyPoints.forEach((keypoints) => {
   drawSegment(
     toTuple(keypoints[0].position), toTuple(keypoints[1].
     position), scale, ctx,
   );
 });
}
```

Last, you will need drawKeypoints() to draw the keypoints. Note that this function and drawSkeleton() check if the confidence of the detected keypoints is above a certain threshold. If not, the method will not return the prediction:

```
export function drawKeypoints(keypoints, minConfidence, ctx,
scale = 1) {
```

```
for (let i = 0; i < keypoints.length; i += 1) {
  const keypoint = keypoints[i];

  if (keypoint.score >= minConfidence) {
    const { y, x } = keypoint.position;
    drawPoint(ctx, y * scale, x * scale, 3);
  }
 }
}
```

With the drawing functions defined, we have what we need to predict the keypoints and show them. So, head back to *index.js* and import *draw.js*:

```
import { drawKeypoints, drawSkeleton } from './draw.js';
```

Now go to `init()`. Right after the line where you called `loadVideo()`, use the following to load the model (make sure you declare `model`):

```
let model;
async function init() {
  const video = await loadVideo();
  model = await posenet.load({
    architecture: 'MobileNetV1',
    outputStride: 16,
    inputResolution: { width: 500, height: 500 },
    multiplier: 0.75,
  });

  detect(video);
}
```

PoseNet's `load()` method takes as an argument a configuration object that tunes several aspects of the model. The most important one is `architecture`, and here you specify whether you want to use MobileNet or ResNet. A second attribute, `outputStride`, sets the output resolution.

The smaller the value is, the largest the output, resulting in a more accurate prediction at the cost of speed—the possible values are 8, 16, or 32. Next is the resolution of the input image (`inputResolution`) and the `multiplier`, an attribute only used by the MobileNet variant to control the depth of the convolutional layers. Again, there is a trade-off here. The larger the value, the larger the size of the layers, meaning more accuracy, but at the cost of speed—the possible values are 0.50, 0.75, 1.0, or 1.01. That is for the model! Now return to `getPose()`.

At the very beginning of `getPose()` (before the lines you previously wrote), call `model.estimateSinglePose()` (remember that we are using the single pose estimator) with arguments `video` and a configuration object that has `flipHorizontal` set to `true`. This attribute mirrors the pose horizontally. Then declare the variable `lastPose` at the top of the file. This variable keeps the last pose inferred by the model, which is the pose the game uses to assess if the user performed what the game instructed. Also, create a const `MIN_CONFIDENCE` and set it to 0.3:

```
let lastPose;
const MIN_CONFIDENCE = 0.3;
```

Again, back to `getPose()`, set to `lastPose` the returned value from `estimateSinglePose()`. Then, after all the methods involving `ctx`, but before `requestAnimationFrame()`, call `drawKeypoints()` and `drawSkeleton`. `getPose()` should now look like this:

```
async function getPose() {
    const pose = await model.estimateSinglePose(video, {
        flipHorizontal: true,
    });
    lastPose = pose;

    ctx.clearRect(0, 0, SIZE, SIZE);
```

```
ctx.save();
ctx.scale(-1, 1);
ctx.translate(-SIZE, 0);
ctx.drawImage(video, 0, 0, SIZE, SIZE);
ctx.restore();

drawKeypoints(pose.keypoints, MIN_CONFIDENCE, ctx);
drawSkeleton(pose.keypoints, MIN_CONFIDENCE, ctx);
requestAnimationFrame(getPose);
}
```

Just in case, make sure that getPose() is within the detect() function.

Now return to the app and reload it. As before, you should see the webcam feed in the center of the page, but now it has the keypoints and skeleton detected by PoseNet. Move around a bit so you can get the feel of the detections. If the stream seems slow, tweak the parameter outputStride. Conversely, if the image shows no lag at all, try a smaller value to increase the model's accuracy.

Before proceeding with the next and final part of the tutorial, let's quickly review the model's output. A PoseNet prediction (Figure 5-4) is an object pose made of two attributes: score and keypoints. The second one, keypoints, corresponds to an array of length 17, where each element is one of the keypoints. These elements contain an object with the keypoint confidence score, the name of the part, and its location. The first attribute of the prediction, score, is the mean of the keypoints' confidences.

```
▼Object 🔋
   score: 0.6949703333461109
 ▼keypoints: Array(17)
   ▼0:
      score: 0.9882120490074158
      part: "nose"
    ▶position: {x: 238.92413342358844, y: 246.3177809532979}
    ▶__proto__: Object
   ▶1: {score: 0.9983976483345032, part: "leftEye", position: {…}}
   ▶2: {score: 0.9991539716720581, part: "rightEye", position: {…}}
   ▶3: {score: 0.9694947600364685, part: "leftEar", position: {…}}
   ▶4: {score: 0.9875234365463257, part: "rightEar", position: {…}}
   ▶5: {score: 0.9644882678985596, part: "leftShoulder", position: {…}}
   ▶6: {score: 0.9921486377716064, part: "rightShoulder", position: {…}}
   ▶7: {score: 0.6948342323303223, part: "leftElbow", position: {…}}
   ▶8: {score: 0.9812084436416626, part: "rightElbow", position: {…}}
   ▶9: {score: 0.5398551225662231, part: "leftWrist", position: {…}}
   ▶10: {score: 0.9633086919784546, part: "rightWrist", position: {…}}
   ▶11: {score: 0.44399240612983704, part: "leftHip", position: {…}}
   ▶12: {score: 0.7263361811637878, part: "rightHip", position: {…}}
   ▶13: {score: 0.17236781120300293, part: "leftKnee", position: {…}}
   ▶14: {score: 0.3554868698120117, part: "rightKnee", position: {…}}
   ▶15: {score: 0.013081061653792858, part: "leftAnkle", position: {…}}
   ▶16: {score: 0.024606075137853622, part: "rightAnkle", position: {…}}
```

Figure 5-4. *A PoseNet prediction object*

Creating the gameplay loop

Take off your machine learning developer hat and put on the video game developer one because, in this part of the exercise, you will build the gameplay loop. As mentioned in the introduction, the game's goal is making you do a random pose before the time runs out. To make the game harder and more enjoyable, after reaching a specific score, the time to pose decreases, and the "inverse" mode activates. While in this mode, the user may have to hide, not show, the instructed keypoint. Let's go.

Back at the global variables section, declare the following ones:

```
let timeToPose = 5;
const MAX_STRIKES = 3;
let gameInterval;

// Game status
let inverseMode = false;
let poseToPerform;
let isInverse;
let score = 0;
let strikes = 0;

const keypointsList = ['nose', 'leftEye', 'rightEye',
'leftEar', 'rightEar', 'leftShoulder', 'rightShoulder',
'leftElbow', 'rightElbow', 'leftWrist', 'rightWrist',
'leftHip', 'rightHip', 'leftKnee', 'rightKnee', 'leftAnkle',
'rightAnkle'];
```

Then create a function named initGame(). Here, you will initialize the score and strike variables, get the game's first pose using nextPose() (defined soon), and display the pose to do on the game interface:

```
function initGame() {
  score = 0;
  strikes = 0;
  document.getElementById('score').innerHTML = `${score}`;
  document.getElementById('strikes').innerHTML = `${strikes}`;
  [poseToPerform] = nextPose();
  document.getElementById('pose-to-match').innerHTML =
  `${poseToPerform}`;
}
```

Next, define another function, nextPose(), which returns two values (in a list): a random keypoint from keypointsList and a flag to specify whether this round applies the inverse rule if the mode is active. Note that if the inverse mode is on, there is only a 33% chance of applying its effect:

```
function nextPose() {
 return [keypointsList[getRandomInt(keypointsList.length)],
 inverseMode && getRandomInt(3) === 0];
}

function getRandomInt(max) {
 return Math.floor(Math.random() * Math.floor(max));
}
```

The next function is verifyPose(). As the name indicates, this one checks if the performed pose is correct. It iterates over the keypoints of lastPose while checking if the confidence of the instructed keypoint is greater than the threshold. If true, the function returns true. On the contrary, if the user shows the keypoint while inverse mode is on, then verifyPose() returns false:

```
function verifyPose() {
 let result = isInverse;
 lastPose.keypoints.forEach((element) => {
   if (poseToPerform === element.part && element.score >=
   MIN_CONFIDENCE) {
     if (!isInverse) {
       result = true;
     } else {
       result = false;
     }
   }
 });

 return result;
}
```

Then comes adjustRules(). This function changes the game mode according to the current score. With the default values, if the game score is 3, timeToPose changes to 2, meaning that the user now has two seconds to pose. Likewise, if the score is 5, the inverse mode gets activated:

```
function adjustRules() {
  switch (score) {
    case 3:
      timeToPose = 2;
      break;
    case 5:
      inverseMode = true;
      break;
    default:
      break;
  }
}
```

Next is updateState(), responsible for increasing the user's score (if result is true) and the strikes (if result is false) and culminating the game if the user's strikes reach MAX_STRIKES. If this happens, the game resets. Moreover, updateState() presents on screen the outcome of the round:

```
function updateState(result) {
  const p = document.getElementById('result-text');
  let text = 'WRONG';
  let textColor = 'RED';
  let isGameOver = false;

  switch (result) {
    case true:
      score += 1;
      document.getElementById('score').innerHTML = `${score}`;
```

```
      text = 'CORRECT';
      textColor = 'GREEN';
      adjustRules();
      break;
    case false:
      strikes += 1;
      document.getElementById('strikes').innerHTML =
      `${strikes}`;

      if (strikes >= MAX_STRIKES) {
        text = 'GAME OVER';
        isGameOver = true;
        resetGame();
      }
      break;
    default:
      break;
  }

  p.innerHTML = text;
  p.style.color = textColor;

  return isGameOver;
}
```

Now comes the important function, initGameLoop():

```
function initGameLoop() {
 let timeleft = timeToPose;
 initGame();

 gameInterval = setInterval(() => {
   if (timeleft < 0) {
     timeleft = timeToPose;
     const result = verifyPose();
```

```
    const isGameOver = updateState(result);
    if (isGameOver) {
      return;
    }

    [poseToPerform, isInverse] = nextPose();
    document.getElementById('pose-to-match').innerHTML =
    `${isInverse ? '~' : ''}${poseToPerform}`;
  }

  document.getElementById('countdown').innerHTML = `${timeleft}`;
  timeleft -= 1;
 }, 1000);
}
```

The function starts by setting timeToPose to timeLeft, followed by calling initGame(). Then comes setInterval(), a JavaScript function that executes a callback function at specified intervals (expressed in milliseconds)—ours executes every second. Let me explain why. An obvious alternative would be calling the function every timeToPose seconds since that is the allocated time. But we want to present a timer on the screen so that the user can see the remaining seconds. Hence, the UI needs to update every second.

The callback first checks if timeLeft (to pose) is less than zero. If it is, it resets the timer, calls verifyPose(), and updates the game state according to the pose outcome. Then, it calls nextPose() to compute the next round's pose and presents the keypoint name on the UI. Then, it updates the UI to reflect the current value of timeLeft, followed by subtracting one from the variable.

Similar to how we initialized the game, we need the means to reset it. The following function, resetGame(), takes care of that. It clears out the text fields and stops the interval:

```
function resetGame() {
 ['pose-to-match', 'countdown', 'result-text', 'score',
'strikes'].forEach((id) => {
   document.getElementById(id).innerHTML = '';
 });
 clearInterval(gameInterval);
}
```

To end the exercise, we need to create the two buttons that start and stop the game; "Start" calls initGameLoop() and "Stop," resetGame():

```
function createButton(innerText, selector, id, listener,
disabled = false) {
 const btn = document.createElement('BUTTON');
 btn.innerText = innerText;
 btn.id = id;
 btn.disabled = disabled;

 btn.addEventListener('click', listener);
 document.querySelector(selector).appendChild(btn);
}

function prepareButtons() {
 createButton('Start', '#buttons-menu', 'start-btn',
   () => initGameLoop());

 createButton('Stop', '#buttons-menu', 'stop-btn',
   () => resetGame());
}
```

Finally, return to `init()` and call `prepareButtons()` between `posenet.load()` and `detect()`:

```
async function init() {
  const video = await loadVideo();
  model = await posenet.load({
    architecture: 'MobileNetV1',
    outputStride: 16,
    inputResolution: { width: 500, height: 500 },
    multiplier: 0.75,
  });

  prepareButtons();
  detect(video);
}
```

Testing the game

Time to play! If you go to the app, you will see the two buttons, "start" and "stop." Click "start." But hurry! Remember, you only have five seconds to present the keypoint. After five correct poses, the time countdown will start at 2 seconds, followed by activating the "inverse" mode once the score reaches 5.

Enjoy the game! If you manage to get a high score, let me know. I would like to see it. :)

Recap

Well, that was entertaining. What did you think? In this chapter, we presented an example of a game that involves a machine learning model as part of its gameplay. Our game, titled *Pose for the Net*, is a movement game where the goal is to match the pose presented by it. The model, PoseNet, is a pose estimator and one of the many pre-trained models TensorFlow.js has to offer. Being a pre-trained model meant that we did not have to go through the process of training it or defining it. None of that. The only thing we needed was one line of code to integrate it into our app.

EXERCISES

1. Extend the app so that it supports the multiple poses estimator and two players using the method estimateMultiplePoses().

2. Replace the model with ResNet.

3. Tweak the parameters and compare the trade-off between speed and accuracy.

4. Fit a k-means model to cluster the coordinates of the keypoints.

5. PoseNet is a versatile model that fits many use cases. So, now it is your turn to build something new. If you need ideas, you could start with tracking keypoint or using a combination of them to track more complicated poses like a sitting or a sleeping position.

CHAPTER 6

Identifying toxic text from a Google Chrome Extension

Online toxicity is an unfortunate, challenging, and unwanted reality of the Internet. Take a stroll down any online comment section, Twitter thread, or multiplayer game, and you will find a piece of obscene and offensive text that will make you say "wow." In those circumstances, there is not much we can do, except for clicking the "report" button and hoping that someone or some magic entity identifies and removes the comment. This chapter addresses this issue. Here, we will build a tool capable of detecting and **classifying toxic content**.

Our next exercise involves using TensorFlow.js' pre-trained toxicity classifier to detect the type of toxicity, for example, insult or obscenity, present in a piece of text, making this the first chapter that features text data. The product you will develop is a **Google Chrome Extension** to identify toxic content from a selected text. Figure 6-1 is a screenshot of the widget. There, under the "selected text" header, is the obviously toxic text "you are a disgusting person," and below, a table containing the seven different categories of toxicity and a label pointing out whether the line falls into that class. In this case, the selected text is classified as an "insult" and "toxic."

© Juan De Dios Santos Rivera 2020
J. Rivera, *Practical TensorFlow.js*, https://doi.org/10.1007/978-1-4842-6273-3_6

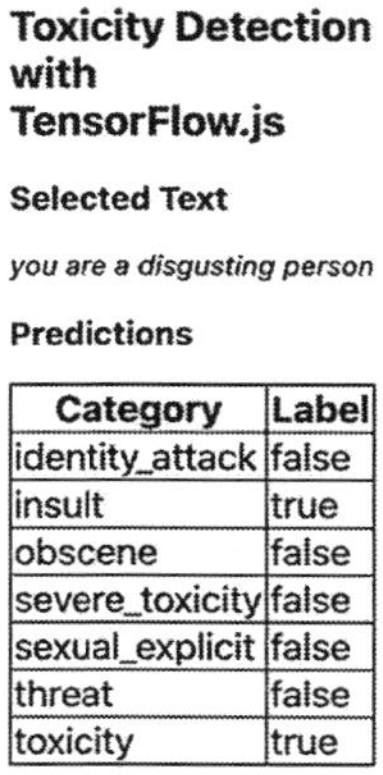

Toxicity Detection with TensorFlow.js

Selected Text

you are a disgusting person

Predictions

Category	Label
identity_attack	false
insult	true
obscene	false
severe_toxicity	false
sexual_explicit	false
threat	false
toxicity	true

Figure 6-1. *A screenshot of the extension*

Understanding the toxicity detector

The toxicity detector model, let's call it **ToxDet**, is a pre-trained model for detecting six subtypes of toxicity content among a piece of (English) text or a series of them. Its six kinds of toxicity—*identity attack, insult, obscene, severe toxicity, sexually explicit, threat*, plus an *overall toxicity* label—cover a significant range or "levels" of vulgarity you would find in an online setting. For example, consider the class "identity attack," which describes "a negative, discriminatory or hateful comment about a person or group of people" (Conversation AI, 2018), or the "threatening" label which identifies text intended to cause harm against an entity or group.

ToxDet is trained on top of another model, known as the **Universal Sentence Encoder** (Cer et al., 2018), or USE, a network that encodes or transforms text into a 512-dimensional embedding. Put differently, USE converts text to an array of 512 floats. To illustrate this, see the following example featuring the TensorFlow.js implementation of USE:[1]

---

[1]https://github.com/tensorflow/tfjs-models/tree/master/universal-sentence-encoder

```
<html>
<head>
  <script src="https://cdn.jsdelivr.net/npm/@tensorflow/tfjs">
  </script>
  <script src="https://cdn.jsdelivr.net/npm/@tensorflow-models/
  universal-sentence-encoder"></script>
</head>
<script>
  use.load().then(model => {
    model.embed('we like tensorflow.js').then(embeddings => {
      embeddings.print(true);
    });
  });
</script>
</html>
```

This example encodes the phrase "we like tensorflow.js" (of course we do) into a tensor of shape [1,512] with values [[-0.0569201, -0.0590669, -0.0376535, …, -0.0493428, 0.0461595, -0.0551419],].

So, how do we go from a model like USE to a toxicity detector? With **transfer learning**. Transfer learning (a technique we will explore in Chapter 8) is the machine learning task of reusing a model originally trained for one problem as a starting point of a second model. Here, the knowledge of USE serves as the base of the toxicity detector. After transferring the knowledge, the resulting new model is further trained with the intended dataset so it can serve its purpose, which is predicting different toxicity categories.

About the data

ToxDet training dataset (Borkan et al., 2019) is a comments corpus from the defunct commenting plugin, *Civil Comments*. This tool featured a comment submission method where, in order to publish a comment, each user first has to review and rate other comments so that others could also rate theirs. The dataset has around 2 million of these rated comments. Its target variable, "target," is a value from 0 to 1 that rates the overall toxicity of the text. Besides having one label, each comment is also ranked in terms of the six subtypes presented earlier. For example, the comment "haha you guys are a bunch of losers" has a target value or toxicity of 0.89, "severe_toxicity" 0.02, "identity_attack" 0.02, and "insult" 0.87.

Because of the generic nature of the data, ToxDet is more suitable for applications of the general domain. Therefore, it might not perform satisfactorily in highly specific use cases or situations when the input data varies significantly from the training set.

Building the extension

By this point, the solutions we have developed involve a web app (or game) where the user interfaces with the model from the browser's window. But a browser is more than just a window. It is also an environment capable of executing small built-in applications that customize the browsing experience and extend its functionalities. One example is the Chrome Extensions, and now you will make one.

The extension is about identifying the subtypes of toxicity present in a selected text using the toxicity model. Using it is very simple. First, the user has to select any text from a web page. With the text selected, it has to click the app's icon to open a small pop-up displaying a table with the predictions (as seen in Figure 6-1). Regarding the implementation, since we will not do any sort of visualization, data processing, training, or even building of a complete UI, the work reduces to loading the model, predicting, and displaying the results. Here we go!

Creating the HTML and app's manifest

We will start this tutorial a bit differently than the others. Instead of creating an *index.html* file, create one named *manifest.json*, a file used to configure the extension. Also, do not worry about the web server; you will not need it. Inside the manifest, set some necessary information such as the name of the extension, version, description, and other more specific attributes:

```
{
  "name": "Toxicity Detection with TensorFlow.js",
  "version": "1.0",
  "description": "Identify Toxic Content",
  "permissions": [
    "activeTab"
  ],
  "browser_action": {
    "default_popup": "src/popup.html"
  },
  "manifest_version": 2,
  "content_security_policy": "script-src 'self' https://cdn.
jsdelivr.net; object-src 'self'"
}
```

The permissions attribute defines the intent of the app. For instance, this extension requires the activeTab permission, one that grants access to the active tab when the user uses the plugin. Another attribute we need is browser_action, used to put icons in the extension's toolbar. Inside it, add a field default_popup and set its value to src/popup.html to open this file after clicking the icon. Two other attributes we use are `manifest_version` to specify the format of the manifest file and `content_security_policy` to allow the app to access `https://cdn.jsdelivr.net`, the CDN from where we have been getting TensorFlow.js. This rule enforces security by ensuring that no other sites can be accessed.

The second file you will need is *popup.html*, the extension interface. In the project's root directory, make an *src/* directory, and within it, create the *popup.html* file. Next, go to the file. There, open a `<head>` tag and import both TensorFlow.js and the toxicity model, and describe the style of the table. Then, in the body, add several headers, a paragraph with `id` attribute `input` to display the selected text, and a table with `id` `predictions-table`. After closing the `<body>` tag, import the extension's main script file, named *popup.js*. And since we are mentioning it, please create the file inside *src/*:

```
<html>
<head>
  <style>
    table,
    td,
    th {
      border: 1px solid black;
    }

    table {
      border-collapse: collapse;
    }
  </style>
  <script src="https://cdn.jsdelivr.net/npm/@tensorflow/
  tfjs"></script>
  <script src="https://cdn.jsdelivr.net/npm/@tensorflow-models/
  toxicity"></script>
</head>
```

```html
<body>
  <h2>Toxicity Detection with TensorFlow.js</h2>
  <h3>Selected Text</h3>
  <p style="font-style: italic;" id="input"></p>
  <h3>Predictions</h3>
  <table id="predictions-table">
    <tr>
      <th>Category</th>
      <th>Label</th>
    </tr>
  </table>
</body>
<script src='popup.js'></script>
</html>
```

The extension script

It will surprise you how small *popup.js* is:

```javascript
const threshold = 0.7;

async function init() {
  const model = await toxicity.load(threshold);

  chrome.tabs.executeScript({
    code: 'window.getSelection().toString();',
  }, async (selection) => {
    const selectedText = selection[0];
    document.getElementById('input').innerHTML = selectedText;
    const table = document.getElementById('predictions-table');
```

```
  await model.classify(selectedText).then((predictions) => {
    predictions.forEach((category) => {
      const row = table.insertRow(-1);
      const labelCell = row.insertCell(0);
      const categoryCell = row.insertCell(1);
      categoryCell.innerHTML = category.results[0].match ===
      null ? '-' : category.results[0].match.toString();
      labelCell.innerHTML = category.label;
    });
  });
});
}

init();
```

The first line sets the prediction threshold, followed by an async function called init(). Inside it, we will load the model using toxicity. load() with the parameter threshold. Afterward comes chrome.tabs. executeScript(), a function from the Chrome Extensions API used to insert and run JavaScript code from the specified tab. Since we are not specifying the tab (in the function's first optional argument), it defaults to the current tab. A second parameter is an object whose attribute code is the code you wish to run, which here is window.getSelection(). toString() to get the selected text. Last, the third parameter is a callback called after the given code is executed; in the callback, we will predict.

The callback function uses as an argument what the window. getSelection().toString() returns—in this case, the selected text, here called selection. In the function's body, get the text from selection's first index, and display it on the app's *input* paragraph. Following it, get the table. Now comes the exciting part, and that is predicting using model. classify().

ToxDet's prediction output is a list of seven objects, where each one represents the toxicity categories. Each of these objects has an attribute label (the toxicity subtype) and results, an array whose values are an object containing the list of probabilities and a boolean match. These probabilities are the likelihood of the text not containing and containing the indicated toxicity target. If the probability of the subtype not appearing is greater than threshold, match is false. Contrarily, if the probability of being present is above threshold, match is true. Otherwise, if none of the scores pass threshold, match is null. In Figure 6-2, you can see an example.

To display the values on the table, iterate over the predictions while appending the label and outcome (if neither probability exceeds the threshold, write a dash). And that's the function! Before moving on, do not forget to call init() from the bottom of the script.

```
▼ (7) [{…}, {…}, {…}, {…}, {…}, {…}, {…}] ⓘ
  ▼ 0:
      label: "identity_attack"
    ▼ results: Array(1)
      ▼ 0:
        ▶ probabilities: Float32Array(2) [0.9122128486633301, 0.0877872034907341]
          match: false
        ▶ __proto__: Object
          length: 1
        ▶ __proto__: Array(0)
      ▶ __proto__: Object
  ▼ 1:
      label: "insult"
    ▼ results: Array(1)
      ▼ 0:
        ▶ probabilities: Float32Array(2) [0.15483859181404114, 0.8451613783836365]
          match: true
        ▶ __proto__: Object
          length: 1
        ▶ __proto__: Array(0)
      ▶ __proto__: Object
  ▶ 2: {label: "obscene", results: Array(1)}
  ▶ 3: {label: "severe_toxicity", results: Array(1)}
  ▶ 4: {label: "sexual_explicit", results: Array(1)}
  ▶ 5: {label: "threat", results: Array(1)}
  ▶ 6: {label: "toxicity", results: Array(1)}
```

Figure 6-2. *An example of a prediction*

Deploying and testing the app

So, how do we deploy this? Easier than it sounds! In Google Chrome, type *chrome://extensions* in the address bar to access the *Extensions Management* page.

On the right side of the screen, use the toggle to enable the "Developer mode." Once activated, click the "LOAD UNPACKED" button (Figure 6-3) and select the extension directory to load the application. Make sure the project's directory follows the following structure:

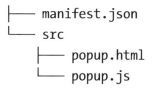

```
├── manifest.json
└── src
    ├── popup.html
    └── popup.js
```

Figure 6-3. *How to activate the "Developer mode"*

After successfully loading the project, you will find the application "T" icon in the extension's toolbar (next to the address bar). If you click it now, the pop-up will show up, but nothing will happen because you have not selected any text. So, select a random line (an obscene one would be appropriate), click the icon, and be amazed by the magic of the model; note that it takes a few seconds to download the model. Table 6-1 presents some examples of offensive text and their toxicity subtypes.

Table 6-1. *Examples of toxic text and their labels*

Text	Identity Attack	Insult	Obscene	Severe Toxicity	Sexual Explicit	Threat
"great game. I enjoyed it"	false	false	false	false	false	false
"your opinion is trash"	false	true	false	false	false	false
"what a moron you f… "	false	true	true	false	false	false

Recap

Besides being a window to the Internet, a web browser is a platform capable of executing small applications that enrich and extend our online journeys. One example is the Google Chrome Extensions, and in this chapter, we have built one. The extension in question uses TensorFlow.js' pre-trained toxicity classifier to identify whether a piece of text has toxic content. With this example, we had the opportunity of applying TensorFlow.js in an environment other than a web application, something that we will keep exploring in Chapter 8, where we will serve a model using Node.js.

Needless to say, let's make the Internet a clean place! Now you have the right tools to get started.

EXERCISES

1. Create a web application where the user inputs the text. To make it even more interesting, classify more than one line during the same call using a list of strings, for example, `model.classify(['lol u silly', 'this is a bad comment'])`.

2. After learning about Node.js in Chapter 8, create a web service that exposes the model. Add an endpoint "predict" that takes as input a string and returns the predictions.

3. Try the Universal Sentence Encoder presented earlier in the chapter. You could start with a simple application that embeds a given text.

4. Use the USE's embeddings to create a dataset of two arbitrary classes of your choice, for example, "sentences about pizza" and "sentences about trees." Then, build a classifier to classify these embeddings.

CHAPTER 7

Object detection with a model trained in Google Cloud AutoML

Deep learning applications for computer vision do not end at image classification, a task we applied in Chapter 4. Back then, our goal was to create an app that identifies a digit drawn by the user. For instance, the digit in Figure 7-1 is a 3.

Figure 7-1. *A number 3*

It's 3, right? Nice. But where is it located? It is right there in the upper-right corner of the picture. Well, that is easy for you to say. But does the computer know that? No, it does not. With the model we have, we can infer

© Juan De Dios Santos Rivera 2020
J. Rivera, *Practical TensorFlow.js*, https://doi.org/10.1007/978-1-4842-6273-3_7

that this is an image of a digit 3. But can it learn precisely where the object is located? Thanks to **object detection**, yes, it can learn that.

Object detection is the machine learning task of identifying an object and so its location within an image or video. For example, a digit detection model would locate the number 3 around the region displayed in Figure 7-2.

Figure 7-2. *The digit's location*

In this chapter, we will create an object detection model, but not for detecting digits. No. Instead, you will detect whatever you want! That's right. For this exercise, I want you to build your dataset using images of two objects—any object.

Unlike the past models you created, you will not train this one in TensorFlow.js. On this occasion, you will take the training to the clouds, specifically to **Google Cloud**, and use their **AutoML Vision Object Detection** service to prepare the dataset and fit the model. Afterward, back on solid ground (your computer), you will build a web application that uses the model to detect the objects in real-time.

Why are we training on an external platform? Good question. The first reason is TensorFlow.js compatibility with the TensorFlow ecosystem. Earlier in the book, we mentioned that being a part of the TensorFlow environment allows TF.js to reuse models trained there, for example, the toxicity detector. So, to experience firsthand this concept of compatibility, the ideal would be to go through the process of training in a TF-related framework such as AutoML and deploy the model in TF.js.

Another reason is that often, in the industry, we encounter situations where we simply cannot train a model on a particular platform. In these cases, the alternative usually is training at one location and deploying in another one.

Reason number three is sharing (is caring). The pre-trained models we have been using are the result of the hard work of an entity that is as passionate about machine learning as we are. So, as a token of appreciation to them, and the rest of the community, let's create a model we could also share with others.

Last, it is always fun learning new frameworks.

What is AutoML Vision Object Detection

AutoML Vision Object Detection is Google Cloud's solution for training and deploying custom object detection models. It offers a graphical interface that allows the user to easily provide its own training data and then train, evaluate, and use models with only a few clicks (no code required), making it ideal for a whole range of people. Along with training, the platform provides a tool to label and annotate the images, the (not-so-fun) task of drawing bounding boxes around the target object. Once trained, Vision Object Detection supports exporting an optimized version of the model for "edge" devices, such as mobile devices and TensorFlow.js.

The service is not free. However, Google offers 40 free node hours that are enough for creating a prototype model.

About the model

A service such as AutoML hides the technicalities and complexities of the system behind a graphical user interface that streamlines many of its processes; click, click, and voila! You got your model (isn't that great?). However, it also means missing out on those small but interesting details, such as the specifications of the model. At the time of writing, the platform documentation does not precisely describe the model or its architecture. It only mentions that it is a "low-latency, high accuracy model(s) optimized for edge devices" (Google, n.d.), a description that matches the MobileNet family of models. Regardless of the type, know that is a small and fast quantized model tailored for platforms like TensorFlow.js and TensorFlow Lite, a framework for mobile device inference.

Note   In TensorFlow, model quantization is a technique that reduces the model size to make it faster at the cost of accuracy. For more information, visit `www.tensorflow.org/lite/performance/post_training_quantization`.

About the data

To train the object detection model, you will need to create an image dataset containing two objects of your choice. Whatever you want. It can be a flower, a pencil, or, as in my case, a Pikachu plushie and a water bottle.

But before you grab your camera and start shooting, here are some tips to consider. First, AutoML recommends at least ten instances of the object; I would suggest at least 50 per label for such a toy project. "But hey author, isn't 50 still a low number?" Yes, you are right. Deep learning models are data-hungry. But, AutoML leverages transfer learning, so you will not have to train a model from scratch.

Regarding the pictures, try to capture the objects from multiple angles (imagine you are a photographer in a photo shoot). Consider shooting the item from different distances. Omit parts of the object in some images— several of my Pikachu images show only its tail. If possible, try various lighting conditions.

Training the model

We will split this exercise into two principal parts: training the model and building the app. In this first part, you will prepare the dataset, train, and export the model.

Setting up your Google Cloud account

To use AutoML Vision Object Detection, you need a Google Cloud account. To avoid sidetracking, we will not discuss here the "how-to" (you can find plenty of documentation online). With the account created, go to `https://console.cloud.google.com/`, and search for "cloud vision api" (Figure 7-3) and select the only result. Then click the "ENABLE" button (Figure 7-4) to authorize the account to use the service. Once enabled, search for "datasets vision" to visit the dataset management screen.

Figure 7-3. *Search for "cloud vision api"*

Figure 7-4. *Enable the API*

Preparing the dataset

This page is about the datasets. Here you can create new datasets or update existing ones. To add one, click the "NEW DATASET" button at the top of the page. This action creates a small window titled "Create new dataset," where you have to specify the name of the dataset and the model objective. Select "Object detection" and click "CREATE DATASET" (Figure 7-5).

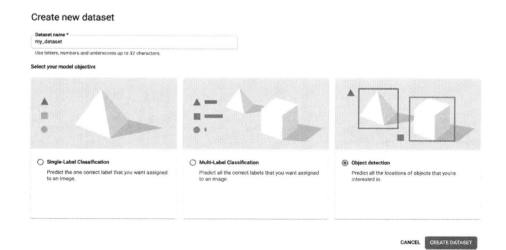

Figure 7-5. *Create a dataset*

On the next screen, select the "Upload images from your computer" option, followed by clicking the "SELECT FILES" button to choose the images. Then pick a Cloud Storage bucket to upload the files. If you do not have a bucket, you can create a new one on the same screen. Now, press "CONTINUE" to upload the images, followed by clicking the "IMAGES" tag. You will probably need to wait a bit until the system processes and stores them.

Labeling and annotating the images

When the images are processed, the next step is labeling and annotating them. In the "IMAGES" tag, click "ADD NEW LABEL" and define the label of your images, for example, "pikachu" (Figure 7-6). Then, click the first photo and draw a bounding box around the object. Repeat the same for the rest of the dataset (have fun!).

Figure 7-6. *Labeling an image*

Training

Are you done with the labeling? Congrats! That was probably the hardest part of the exercise. Now let's proceed with the training. To start, go to the "TRAIN" tab, and click the "TRAIN NEW MODEL" button. In the new window, you need to define several attributes regarding the model. The first is the name. Then is the deployment target—choose "Edge." In point number two, select "Best trade-off" (Figure 7-7) to have both a fast and good model or whichever suits your needs. Last, set the node hour budget. The recommended value should be enough. Now click "START TRAINING" to start. With around 100 images, the training can take approximately two hours.

	Goal	Package size	Accuracy	Latency for Google Pixel 2
○	Higher accuracy	2.8 MB	Higher	360 ms
◉	Best trade-off	2.8 MB	Medium	150 ms
○	Faster predictions	2.8 MB	Lower	56 ms

Figure 7-7. *Select the model type*

Evaluate

Welcome back. Let's see how the training went. Back in the management screen, go to the "EVALUATE" tab. During training, AutoML automatically separates part of the dataset for evaluating the model. Here, you will find the results. The evaluation metrics are the precision and recall at a particular confidence level and **Intersect over Union** or IoU threshold level.

The IoU is a score that measures the area of overlap between the object's predicted position and the ground truth, divided by the area of the union. Figure 7-8 presents an example of a good IoU and a bad one. The left example is a good IoU because the predicted bounding box (dotted line) almost overlaps the ground truth box completely, while the right one is bad because the detection is nowhere near the actual position.

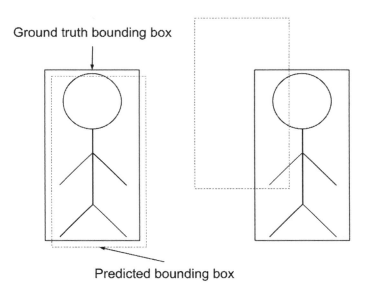

Figure 7-8. *Examples of IoU*

Clicking the label name shows the true positives (cases when the model correctly predicted the bounding box), false negatives (when the model did not predict an accurate bounding box), and false positives (when the model predicted an incorrect bounding box) cases and the predicted and ground truth boundaries (Figure 7-9). How did the training go? Are you satisfied with the results? If not, you could try adding more images to the training set and selecting the high-accuracy model variant. Otherwise, proceed by clicking the "TEST & USE" tab.

bottle

Total images	127
Test items	8
Total objects	8
Object to image avg	1
Precision ❔	100%
Recall ❔	87.5%

Use the slider to see which confidence threshold works best for your model on the precision-recall tradeoff curve.
Learn more about these metrics and graphs.

All test images are evaluated at the time of training. If you modify your dataset after training, these results will not be accurate.

True positives

Your model correctly predicted bottle on these images

▨ Predicted   ▨ Ground Truth

Score: 0.9849337

Figure 7-9. *The "evaluate" tab*

Exporting the model

Now comes the last step, and that is exporting the model. From this screen, you can export different optimized versions of the model capable of running on platforms, like TensorFlow.js and TFLite. Click the "TensorFlow.js" option. In the pop-up window, select a GCS bucket and click "EXPORT" to save the model in that location. To download the files to your computer, you can use the command shown on the screen or click "OPEN IN GCS" to access the bucket and get them from there. If you opt for the first option, create the local destination folder before running the command:

```
$ mkdir model
$ gsutil cp -r gs://model-bucket model/
```

Regardless of the method you choose, you should at least have three files:

1. A dict.txt (the labels)

2. A model.json (the model's specifications)

3. Several *.bin files (the model's weights)

With that, we finish the training phase. Did you enjoy the journey? Hope so!

Building the app

Close the cloud console and return to our local environment. In this section, you will write an app that imports the model and performs real-time object detection on the webcam feed. The app has a canvas that shows the video and the prediction bounding boxes and three sliders to control the prediction rate. As usual, create a new directory and the *index. html*, *index.js*, and *style.css* files, and copy the model's directory here. The directory structure should be as follows:

```
├── index.html
├── index.js
├── model
│   ├── dict.txt
│   ├── group1-shard1of3.bin
│   ├── group1-shard2of3.bin
│   ├── group1-shard3of3.bin
│   └── model.json
└── style.css
```

Loading packages and preparing the UI

At the top of *index.html*, use two script tags to import TensorFlow.js, *AutoML Edge API*[1] (tfjs-automl), and the CSS file. This AutoML library is a collection of tools to load and execute edge models produced in Google Cloud's AutoML:

```
<html>
<head>
 <script src="https://cdn.jsdelivr.net/npm/@tensorflow/tfjs">
 </script>
 <script src="https://cdn.jsdelivr.net/npm/@tensorflow/tfjs-
 automl"></script>
 <link href="./style.css" rel="stylesheet">
</head>
</html>
```

After `<head>`, create the app's `<body>` and, in it, the `<video>`, `<canvas>`, and three "sliders" (`<input>` of type range). The first of these ranges, `score-range`, takes a value between 0 and 1 that controls the prediction's minimum confidence threshold. Range `iou-range` adjusts the model's Intersection over Union threshold to ignore predicted boxes with IoU lower than the score. `topk-range` handles how many objects a prediction returns by selecting the `topk` bounding boxes with the highest confidence scores. Then, call *index.js* using a `<script>` tag:

```
<body>
  <div class="main-centered-container">
    <h2>Detect your objects!</h2>
    <div id="menu" class="flex-ui">
```

---

[1]https://npmjs.com/package/@tensorflow/tfjs-automl

```html
    <form>
      <h4>Score threshold:</h4>
      <input type="range" id="score-range" min="0" max="1"
      value="0.5" step="0.01">
      <p><span id="score-value"></span></p>
      <h4>IoU threshold:</h4>
      <input type="range" id="iou-range" min="0" max="1"
      value="0.5" step="0.05">
      <p><span id="iou-value"></span></p>
      <h4>Top k:</h4>
      <input type="range" id="topk-range" min="1" max="20"
      value="1">
      <p><span id="topk-value"></span></p>
    </form>
    <div>
      <video id="video" playsinline style="display: none;">
      </video>
      <canvas id="output" />
    </div>
  </div>
  <script src="index.js"></script>
 </div>
</body>
```

Last, copy the following CSS code—to align the elements—in *style.css*:

```css
.main-centered-container {
  padding-left: 60px;
  padding-right: 60px;
  margin: 0 auto;
  max-width: 1280px;
}
```

```
.flex-ui {
  display: flex;
  flex-wrap: wrap;
}

.flex-ui div {
  flex: 1;
  padding: 20px;
  text-align: center;
}
```

Importing the model and setting up the camera

Close *index.html* and head over to *index.js*. Similar to the PoseNet app, this exercise's implementation involves setting up a canvas to display the webcam feed and the model's predictions.

Start by declaring the canvas context (ctx) variable and the size:

```
let ctx;
const SIZE = 500;
```

Then, use the following two functions, setupCamera() and loadVideo() (they are the same we used in the PoseNet app):

```
function setupCamera() {
  const video = document.getElementById('video');
  video.width = SIZE;
  video.height = SIZE;

  navigator.mediaDevices.getUserMedia({
    audio: false,
    video: {
      width: SIZE,
      height: SIZE,
    },
```

```
  }).then((stream) => {
    video.srcObject = stream;
  });

  return new Promise((resolve) => {
    video.onloadedmetadata = () => resolve(video);
  });
}

async function loadVideo() {
  const video = await setupCamera();
  video.play();

  return video;
}
```

Now for the init() function. In the first line, use the loadObjectDetection() function from *tfjs-automl* to load the model using as an argument the path to *model.json*. Next, call loadVideo(). Use both returned values as arguments to the detect() function, which we will define next:

```
async function init() {
  const model = await tf.automl.loadObjectDetection('model/
  model.json');
  const video = await loadVideo();
  detect(model, video);
}
```

Detecting the objects

The next function we will set up is detect(), the one that performs the predictions and adds the webcam video to the canvas:

```
let scoreThreshold = 0.95;
let iouThreshold = 0.5;
let topkThreshold = 10;

function detect(model, video) {
  const canvas = document.getElementById('output');
  ctx = canvas.getContext('2d');

  canvas.width = SIZE;
  canvas.height = SIZE;

  async function getBoundingBoxes() {
    const predictions = await model.detect(video, {
      score: scoreThreshold,
      iou: iouThreshold,
      topk: topkThreshold,
    });

    ctx.save();
    ctx.scale(-1, 1);
    ctx.translate(-SIZE, 0);
    ctx.drawImage(video, 0, 0, SIZE, SIZE);
    ctx.restore();

    predictions.forEach((prediction) => {
      drawBoundingBoxes(prediction);
    });
```

```
    requestAnimationFrame(getBoundingBoxes);
  }

  getBoundingBoxes();
}
```

Start the function by getting the canvas and its context and setting the width and height to SIZE. Inside the function, create another one and name it getBoundingBoxes(). Here, call the model's detect() method using as arguments the video stream and an options object to configure the detection parameters score, iou, and topk. Note that we declared the options' default values above the function; if you prefer, you could move them to the top of the file next to the other variables.

The method model.detect() returns a list of predictions object (Figure 7-10), where each of these has three attributes: box, label, and score. box is the bounding box or the position of the identified object. It has four values: left, top, width, and height, where left and top are the locations of the box top-left corner in the x-axis and y-axis, and width and height are the box dimensions. Following box is label, or the class of the object, and the prediction score.

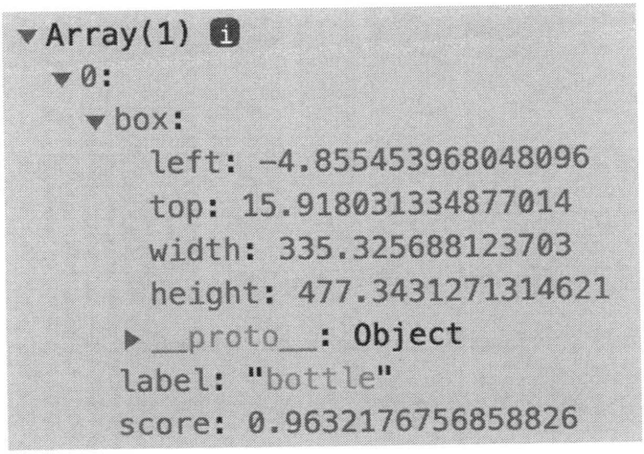

```
▼ Array(1)  ℹ
  ▼ 0:
    ▼ box:
        left: -4.855453968048096
        top: 15.918031334877014
        width: 335.325688123703
        height: 477.3431271314621
      ▶ __proto__: Object
      label: "bottle"
      score: 0.9632176756858826
```

Figure 7-10. *A prediction object*

After predicting, the next step involves using `ctx` to draw the webcam feed. To overlay the bounding boxes, we must iterate over the predictions array and call `drawBoundingBoxes()` (we will see it in the next section) on each prediction. Last, call `requestAnimationFrame()` and `getBoundingBoxes()` from detect.

Drawing the bounding boxes

With the camera and predictions ready, the only missing part is visualizing them on screen. The next function we will see is `drawBoundingBoxes()`, responsible for overlaying the predicted bounding boxes on top of the object. Besides the boxes, the overlay includes the object's label and confidence score.

```
const BBCOLOR = '#3498eb';
function drawBoundingBoxes(prediction) {
  ctx.font = '20px Arial';
  const {
    left, top, width, height,
  } = prediction.box;

  ctx.strokeStyle = BBCOLOR;
  ctx.lineWidth = 1;
  ctx.strokeRect(left, top, width, height);

  ctx.fillStyle = BBCOLOR;
  const textWidth = ctx.measureText(prediction.label).width;
  const textHeight = parseInt(ctx.font, 10);

  ctx.fillRect(left, top, textWidth + textHeight,
  textHeight * 2);
  ctx.fillRect(left, top + height - textHeight * 2,
  textWidth + textHeight, textHeight * 2);
```

```
ctx.fillStyle = '#000000';
ctx.fillText(prediction.label, left, top + textHeight);
ctx.fillText(prediction.score.toFixed(2), left, top +
height - textHeight);
}
```

Testing the app

We are almost there. The only thing we are missing is creating a function
that handles the slider's input updates:

```
function updateSliders(metric, updateAttribute) {
  const slider = document.getElementById(`${metric}-range`);
  const output = document.getElementById(`${metric}-value`);
  output.innerHTML = slider.value;
  updateAttribute(slider.value);

  slider.oninput = function oninputCb() {
    output.innerHTML = this.value;
    updateAttribute(this.value);
  };
}
```

updateSliders() has two parameters. The first one, (the metric)
name, corresponds to the prediction's attribute we wish to update, for
example, topk. The second parameter, updateAttribute, is the callback
function executed whenever the user changes the slider's value. The
function's role is updating the value of the given variable. Also, we will use
updateAttribute to set the slider's initial values too.

After defining the function, return to init and use updateSliders()
three times, one for each of the options values (score, iou, and topk).
Then, call init():

```
async function init() {
  const model = await tf.automl.loadObjectDetection('model/
  model.json');
  const video = await loadVideo();
  detect(model, video);

  updateSliders('score', (value) => {
    scoreThreshold = parseFloat(value);
  });

  updateSliders('iou', (value) => {
    iouThreshold = parseFloat(value);
  });

  updateSliders('topk', (value) => {
    topkThreshold = parseInt(value, 10);
  });
}

init();
```

Now to try the app. Back at the terminal, use *http-server* to start the
local server, followed by launching the application. Then, after a few
seconds (while the app reads the model and sets the webcam), pick up
your objects, and show them to the camera. If everything went as planned,
you should see the detections.

In terms of accuracy, the model we just trained is not the best nor as good as the others we have seen or trained in the past chapters. As we discussed earlier, being an edge model means trading much of its prediction power for gains in speed, a feature that is well received in this application. Another reason is the lack of data. If you followed the instructions, your training set has around 100 images, which for such a model is very low. But luckily for us, we can always add examples to the dataset and create new versions of the model. So, if you enjoyed annotating the images, you will love the second exercise of this chapter.

As a quick remedy to handle the false positives (my model labeled me as "pikachu," which I do not mind at all) and false negatives, try experimenting with the object's position, for example, the angle. Another alternative is tweaking the prediction's attributes to control their flexibility. A lower threshold score produces more predictions at the cost of introducing more errors, while a high one gives fewer mistakes but also fewer detections.

Recap

In this chapter, we went on a trip to the (Google) cloud to train a model using AutoML Vision Object Detection, a service for developing and deploying machine learning models. Up there, after going through the amusing procedure of annotating and labeling a dataset, we trained an object detection model within a few clicks. Then, we built an object detection web application that uses the trained model and the webcam to detect in real-time the objects presented during training. While doing so, we experienced firsthand the compatibility that TensorFlow.js has with other platforms.

You can find my model in the book's GitHub repository.

EXERCISES

1.   What is object detection?

2.   Add more training examples (try around 500 images per label).

3.   Train the high-performance or the faster model (depending on which you used) and compare their speed and predictions.

4.   Extend the web app with a module that detects objects from images.

5.   Build a Chrome extension that uses the app to detect objects from online images.

6.   For the adventurous, export the TFLite version of the model and deploy it in an Android device using this tutorial: `https://cloud.google.com/vision/automl/docs/tflite-android-tutorial`.

7.   Share the model on GitHub, and with me! I'd love to see what you built.

CHAPTER 8

Training an image classifier with transfer learning on Node.js

An intersection between the products we have so far built—a game, a web application, or a Chrome extension—is that they live in the browser. From this ecosystem, we have trained models, loaded others, visualized data, detected mean words, and more. But the reality is different. Unlike our apps, most of the models we interact with every day are in a server, and not client-side. There, from the server, we deploy and expose machine learning models to the users through a service. In this chapter, we will create one.

Using **Node.js**, a runtime environment that executes JS code outside the browser, we will develop a server-side application for deploying and serving a TensorFlow.js model via a web service. But which model?

Before creating the service—let's call it the *Server*—you will write another Node.js program (the *Trainer*) for training an image classifier using the personalized dataset from Chapter 7. However, instead of training it from scratch, you will apply **transfer training** to a pre-trained **MobileNet** model and start from there.

© Juan De Dios Santos Rivera 2020
J. Rivera, *Practical TensorFlow.js*, https://doi.org/10.1007/978-1-4842-6273-3_8

Wow, so many concepts: Node.js, servers, web services, transfer learning, and MobileNet. Well, there is another one! To inspect the training, we will use **TensorBoard**,[1] a TensorFlow visualization toolkit that, among other features, provides tracking of the model's performance metrics and loss values.

What is transfer learning?

Training a (large) deep learning model is a computationally extensive task that requires a vast amount of data. To get an idea, NVIDIA's *Megatron-LM* (Shoeybi et al., 2019), an 8.3 billion parameter transformer model, required two days per epoch using 512 GPUs. Two days! Per epoch! I do not know about you, but I do not own that kind of hardware. So, how can we, ordinary people, train deep models in a relatively short time and with a limited dataset? An option is transfer learning.

Transfer learning refers to the technique of reusing parts (the trained weights) of a model as a starting point of another. In other words, it *transfers the knowledge learned in one setting to another* (Goodfellow et al., 2016). Using a pre-trained model as a base to a second one implies significantly speeding up the training of the target model and requiring less training data.

The main idea behind transfer learning consists of concatenating the base model's layers to a new set of layers and training them. In practice, this involves using the upper layers (the first layers) of the base model since they are most likely to have learned the high-level features of their dataset, that is, these features are the ones that might be useful for the new model. These layers are sometimes known as "frozen" layers because their weights are fixed and will not be trained. To these frozen layers, then, you append the new set of layers, including the output layer, and train these

---

[1]https://tensorflow.org/tensorboard

with your data to create the relationship between what the base model knows and the target of your dataset.

As useful as transfer learning is, it is not a perfect or a "one-size-fits-all" solution. When applying it, there are several things we must consider. One is the layer from which we should "truncate" the model, a decision that depends on the size of the training set; the more data you have, the higher the cutting point (less frozen layers) (Géron, 2019). Another possible issue is the similarity between the task of the original model and the model we want to train. For example, if the original model is for detecting potatoes, you cannot expect that it will be good at identifying spaceships (unless they are potato-shaped spaceships). Therefore, try using a base model trained on a similar dataset or a large and diverse one, such as ImageNet. Similarly, we need to keep in mind the input shape of the base model. For instance, our base model, MobileNet, is trained on images of size 224x224, so we have to resize our dataset before feeding it to the model.

Understanding MobileNet and ImageNet

Our base model is a MobileNet (Howard et al., 2017), a light and fast convolutional neural network architecture for visual applications, which include object detection, image classification, and novel ones like the PoseNet network from Chapter 5. MobileNet targets low-resource devices such as embedded systems and mobile phones, which is why it trades accuracy for speed. It has over 25 layers, which include a special convolutional layer named depthwise separable convolution as well as batch normalization layers, ReLU activation layers, a convolutional layer, and a softmax layer for classification.

The MobileNet model we will use was trained on the *ImageNet Large Scale Visual Recognition Challenge 2012* (ILSVRC2012) database (Russakovsky et al., 2015) where it achieved an accuracy of 70.6%. The dataset has 1,431,167 images and 1000 classes that depict items, animals, and objects, among others, for example, "football," "helmet," "candle," "eel," and "digital clock." If the labels seem all over the place, it is because this dataset is a subset of the larger ImageNet, which aims to cover most nouns of the English language. Having a model trained with such a mix of a diverse object might be beneficial for our transfer learning job.

Building the Trainer

Our first task is creating the Trainer, responsible for training the model. This program does two things, pre-processing the data and training the model, and so we will split the explanation into two parts. Besides, since we have a new framework, Node.js, we will start with a brief description of how to run TensorFlow.js in this environment.

Setting up the environment

The first step is installing Node.js. You can find the instructions at https://nodejs.org/en/. Installing Node.js also installs **npm**, a package manager for JavaScript projects. Once ready, add a directory in your preferred location and create the file *package.json*, a document with metadata about the project. Ours looks like this:

```
{
  "name": "tfjs-node-trainer-server",
  "version": "0.0.1",
  "description": "Train a image classifier using transfer
  learning and deploy it",
  "scripts": {
    "train": "node trainer.js",
    "serve": "node server.js",
    "tensorboard": "tensorboard --logdir /tmp/fit_logs"
  },
```

```
"dependencies": {
  "@tensorflow/tfjs-node": "^1.5.2",
  "express": "^4.17.1",
  "multer": "^1.4.2"
}
}
```

The first three keys are the project's name, version, and description. Then comes the `scripts` property, a dictionary of commands. For example, we have a `train` command whose value is `node trainer.js`, so executing `npm train` in the path where *package.json* is runs `node trainer.js`. The next attribute defines the project's dependencies, which are Node.js version of TensorFlow.js, *Express* and *Multer*, two we will use for the web service. If your computer has an NVIDIA GPU and supports CUDA, you could instead use the GPU variant, *tfjs-node-gpu*.

To make sure everything is working, first, run `npm i` to install the dependencies. When that finishes, create a file named *trainer.js*, add the line `console.log('boo!');`, and execute `npm run train` from the console.

Loading and pre-processing the images

Did it work? Cool. Now, remove the "boo" line and replace it with the following two to load TensorFlow.js and the *fs* (short for "File System") module:

```
const tf = require('@tensorflow/tfjs-node');
// or const tf = require('@tensorflow/tfjs-node-gpu');
const fs = require('fs');
```

Right after, declare these three variables:

```
const NUM_CLASSES = 2;
let xTrain;
let yTrain;
```

where xTrain is the dataset and yTrain the labels.

Next, create readImage(). The function consists of one call to tf. tidy(), to read images from the file system using *fs*' readFileSync(), followed by tf.node.decodeImage() to decode it and convert to a tensor. Next, transform the tensor using the following methods:

- resizeBilinear([224, 224]) to resize it to 224x224. After this function, the tensor's shape is [224, 224, 3]. The 3 is because of the colored image RGB channels.

- expandDims() to add an extra dimension. Tensor shape: [1, 224, 224, 3].

- toFloat() to convert the values to floats.

- div(127.0) to divide the values by 127.

- sub(1) to subtract 1. These last two methods bound the values between -1 and 1 (RGB values range from 0 to 255).

To avoid keeping these intermediate tensors in memory, wrap up everything inside a tf.tidy():

```
function readImage(path) {
  return tf.tidy(() => {
    const imageBuffer = fs.readFileSync(path);
    const tfimage = tf.node.decodeImage(imageBuffer);
    return tfimage.resizeBilinear([224, 224])
      .expandDims()
      .toFloat()
      .div(127.0)
      .sub(1);
  });
}
```

The script's second function is getImages(). This one takes two parameters, dir, a directory containing images, and label, the dataset's labels, coded as numbers, for example, 0 for "pikachu." getImages() uses *fs* method readdir() and a foreach to iterate over a directory's files that are used by the function readImages() to get the images. After each image, it calls tf.oneHot() to create a *one-hot* tensor that encodes the image's class. A one-hot vector is a vector of length n, where $n − 1$ values are zero, and the remaining one is 1. In machine learning, we frequently use this technique to label datasets in such a way where only the index corresponding to the instance's class is 1, while the others are 0. For example, suppose that in our "pikachu and bottle" classifier, the index of class "pikachu" is 0, and that of "bottle" is 1. Here, the one-hot encoding of a "bottle" label is [0, 1].

With the image and label set, the missing step is concatenating them to xTrain and yTrain along the first axis, that is, to form a tensor of images:

```
async function getImages(dir, label) {
  let img;
  let y;

  fs.readdir(dir, (_, files) => {
    files.forEach(async (file) => {
      img = readImage(`${dir}/${file}`);
      y = tf.tidy(() => tf.oneHot(tf.tensor1d([label]).toInt(),
      NUM_CLASSES));

      if (xTrain == null) {
        xTrain = img;
        yTrain = y;
      } else {
        xTrain = xTrain.concat(img, 0);
        yTrain = yTrain.concat(y, 0);
      }
```

```
    });
  });

  tf.dispose(img);
  tf.dispose(y);
}
```

Training the model with transfer learning

Welcome to transfer learning! After repeating the term so many times, you must be (maybe) eager to apply it. So, let's start right away with a new function named `train()`. The function's first commands involve using the method `tf.loadLayersModel()` to load a version of MobileNet provided by Google and `tf.LayersModel.getLayer()` to get the layer "conv_pw_13_relu."

This "conv_pw_13_relu" layer is the cutting point. All the layers before this one are considered "frozen," that is, they are the "learning" we will transfer (the base model). Why this particular layer? One reason is its proximity to the output layer—meaning that we will use many learned layers—and because it performed well with my dataset. However, you do not have to choose the same one. After we finish building the model, I would recommend trying different cutting points to see which one is better for your data.

```
async function train() {
  const mobilenet = await tf.loadLayersModel('https://storage.
  googleapis.com/tfjs-models/tfjs/mobilenet_v1_0.25_224/model.
  json');

  const cutoffLayer = mobilenet.getLayer('conv_pw_13_relu');
}
```

Note   Use `mobilenet.summary()` to see the network's layers name.

Since we know the cutting point, let's get the corresponding layers and build a new model with them. This model is not a sequential one, but a graph-based one that uses the functional approach we saw back in Chapter 1. To create it, we will use the property inputs and outputs of the argument object to set its inputs and outputs (write this under the `cutoffLayer` line):

```
const truncatedModel = tf.model({
    inputs: mobilenet.inputs,
    outputs: cutoffLayer.output,
});
```

If you are curious, run `console.log(mobilenet.summary())` and `console.log(truncatedModel.summary())` to see the difference in the architecture.

The following step is producing the intermediate activations using `truncatedModel.predict(xTrain)`. Mind that this is not "predicting" in the sense that we are used to because there is no classification output. Here, we are using the weights of the base model to produce an intermediate activation tensor used by the second model:

```
const activation = truncatedModel.predict(xTrain);
```

Now create the final model that takes the activation tensor as input and produces the image classification. The model needs three layers. The first of these is a flatten layer, whose `inputShape` is the shape of `truncatedModel`'s output. The following is a dense layer of 20 units and a ReLU activation function. As for the last one, add another dense layer where units equal `NUM_CLASSES`, and the activation function is softmax.

Then compile it using the categorical cross-entropy loss function, an Adam optimizer with a learning rate of 0.001, and the accuracy metric.

To fit the model, this time, we will use a new callback tf.node. tensorBoard(). This callback writes the training's metric and loss values in the directory specified in the function's argument. Later, with TensorBoard, we will read these logs to track the training process. As for the other parameters, use the activation tensor as training data, the label yTrain, and a configuration object to set the batch size to 32 and epochs to 15. Last, use model.save() to save the model:

```
const model = tf.sequential();

model.add(tf.layers.flatten(
  { inputShape: truncatedModel.output.shape.slice(1) },
));

model.add(tf.layers.dense({
  units: 20,
  activation: 'relu',
}));

model.add(tf.layers.dense({
  units: NUM_CLASSES,
  activation: 'softmax',
}));

model.compile({
  loss: 'categoricalCrossentropy',
  optimizer: tf.train.adam(0.001),
  metrics: ['accuracy'],
});
```

```
await model.fit(activation, yTrain, {
  batchSize: 32,
  epochs: 15,
  callbacks: tf.node.tensorBoard('/tmp/fit_logs'),
});

await model.save('file://model/');
```

That's it for `train()`. You can close the function.

Running the Trainer

To complete the script, define the starting point with an `init()` function:

```
async function init() {
  await getImages('data/pikachu/', 0);
  await getImages('data/bottle/', 1);
  train();
}
init();
```

Note that you need one call to `getImages()` per class. Their arguments are the path to a directory that should only contain images of one class and the label (as a number). If you have all the pictures under the same directory, please split them into two.

Back at the terminal, open a second tab and run `pip install tensorboard` to install TensorBoard. Once installed, execute `npm run tensorboard` and click the given address (probably `http://localhost:6006`) to launch the tool. From the terminal's first tab, run `npm run train` to initiate the training script. The program needs about one minute to load and process all the images. While this happens, if you trace the computer's memory usage, you will see how it fills up a bit and drops after the dispose methods.

Note   pip is a Python package manager. To learn how to install it, visit `https://pip.pypa.io/en/stable/installing/`.

During the training, once you spot the log messages on the terminal, switch to TensorBoard (Figure 8-1) to track the accuracy and loss. If they are not there, either wait a few seconds until the Trainer writes the log or click the refresh button.

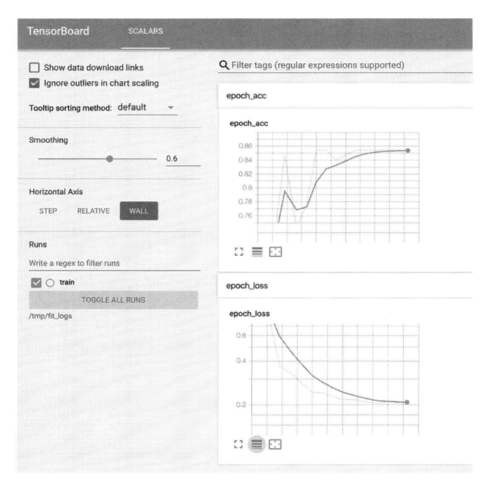

Figure 8-1. *TensorBoard*

Note   If you re-train, change the TensorBoard log directory on the callback or make sure it is empty. Otherwise, you will have logs from different trainings.

With my dataset, the model achieved an accuracy of 0.85 and a loss of 0.207 after ten epochs (not a terrible result). If you are not happy with yours, you could try several things starting with adjusting the hyperparameters' learning rate, units, or the number of epochs. Another alternative is trying fewer layers of the base model (in this case, you might need to increase the size of the training set), adding more, or even changing the architecture of the top model.

Building the Server

So, we have a nice model trained with transfer learning, but no way to interact with it. Until now. In this second part of the exercise, we will write the Server, a small Node.js program that exposes the model using a REST web service. Once deployed, you will be able to perform predictions (and see the response) with POST requests sent from the terminal.

Serving the model

Create a new file and name it *server.js*. Then, import TensorFlow.js and two libraries—Express and Multer—that will help us build the web server. After the imports, create a function named `imageBufferToTensor()` to convert an `imageBuffer` to tensor. The function is the same `readImage()` as earlier but without the `fs.readFileSync()` line.

```
const tf = require('@tensorflow/tfjs-node');
const express = require('express');
```

```
const multer = require('multer');

function imageBufferToTensor(imageBuffer) {
  return tf.tidy(() => {
    const tfimage = tf.node.decodeImage(imageBuffer);
    return tfimage.resizeBilinear([224, 224])
      .expandDims()
      .toFloat()
      .div(127)
      .sub(1);
  });
}
```

Below it, define the function that creates and executes the server, runServer():

```
async function runServer() {
  const model = await tf.loadLayersModel('file://model/model.
  json');
  const mobilenet = await tf.loadLayersModel('https://storage.
  googleapis.com/tfjs-models/tfjs/mobilenet_v1_0.25_224/model.
  json');

  const cutoffLayer = mobilenet.getLayer('conv_pw_13_relu');
  const truncatedModel = tf.model({ inputs: mobilenet.inputs,
  outputs: cutoffLayer.output });

  const app = express();
  const storage = multer.memoryStorage();
  const upload = multer({ storage });

  app.post('/upload', upload.single('data'), (req, res) => {
    const img = imageBufferToTensor(req.file.buffer);
    const activation = truncatedModel.predict(img);
    const prediction = model.predict(activation).dataSync();
```

```
  res.json({
    prediction,
  });
});
app.listen(8081, () => {
  console.log('Ready');
});
}

runServer();
```

In the function's first line, we load our model and MobileNet. As before, we have to use a truncated version of MobileNet to create the intermediate activation tensors. After loading the models, set up the web server with Express and use Multer's memoryStorage() function to keep the uploaded images in memory.

Now we create the POST route. This route has a function called the *handler function* that runs when the application receives a request to the specified endpoint, for example, a POST request sent to http://localhost:8081/upload. The function takes two parameters, req (request) and res (response). req is an object containing information about the request, including the data, or in this case, the image, while res is the response we will send back to the user.

This response is the prediction outcome, wrapped in a JSON object. To get it, we need three steps: convert the image buffer to tensor, produce the intermediate activation tensor, and classify it. To end the script, use app.listen() to listen for the requests in the specified port.

Testing the model

To test the model, return to the terminal and execute `npm run serve` to initialize the server. In another terminal tab (once the server is ready), run

```
$ curl -F "data=@data/{DIR_NAME}/{IMAGE_NAME}" http://
localhost:8081/upload
```

where `DIR_NAME` is the directory and `IMAGE_NAME` is the image you want to classify, for example:

```
$ curl -F "data=@data/bottle/0001.jpg" http://localhost:8081/
upload
```

The result is the model prediction encoded as JSON, like this:

```
{"prediction":{"0":0.000023536138542112894,"1":0.99997651576
99585}}
```

It might not look like much, but this service might serve as the starting point of a bigger project. To mention some ideas, you could consider deploying it in a remote server so you can predict from anywhere you want. Or imagine having a client, for example, a web app, that sends images to the server and tidily presents the outcome. It sounds fun. What do you think?

Recap

A TensorFlow.js application is not limited to live in the browser. With the right tools, namely, Node.js and TF.js' own "node" backend mode, we can build hardware-accelerated software for training and deploying models in a server-side program. In this chapter, we explored the Node.js version of TensorFlow.js to create an app that trains a model and a service that serves it. The training script, adequately named the Trainer, uses transfer learning—a technique that transfers the knowledge of one model to another—to fit an image classifier using a limited amount of data. While training, we had a glimpse at TensorBoard—TensorFlow's visualization toolkit—for monitoring the procedure. Our second application, Server, loads the Trainer's model and exposes it with a web service.

Running TensorFlow.js under the Node.js runtime does more than just making it faster. It also provides a unique set of functionalities that allows us to do things such as decoding images, writing logs for TensorBoard, and accelerating the processes even further with its GPU version.

EXERCISES

1. Empirically speaking, how does the object detection model from Chapter 7 compare to this one?

2. Cut the base model at different layers and then perform transfer learning. Did you achieve better results? Worse?

3. Tweak the model's hyperparameters.

4. For experimentation, can you achieve an acceptable accuracy using fewer training samples? The goal is to study how the base model performs on your dataset without seeing much of it.

5. Train a model from scratch. Does it perform better than the one just did here? How many epochs did it need before achieving the same accuracy?

6. For the curious, open `model.json` and study the complete topology of the model.

7. Share the model!

CHAPTER 9

Time series forecasting and text generation with recurrent neural networks

Think of your morning routine. You wake up, grab your phone, and check your messages, emails, and others. Minutes after, you go to the bathroom, take a shower, and brush your teeth (maybe while showering?). After those blissful minutes under the water, you get breakfast, probably a coffee, and get ready to seize the day. Those are the basics. Now, look back at this list and tell me, does it resemble a **sequence**? It sure looks like one. If so, would it be possible to predict the next step(s) using past actions as the predictors? With the right model, yes.

A machine learning architecture capable of predicting or anticipating the future is the **recurrent neural network** (RNN). These networks take as input a sequence of arbitrary length and try to predict the next action. Generally speaking, RNNs can predict many steps in the future, allowing us to know not just what comes after current timestep t but also what

© Juan De Dios Santos Rivera 2020
J. Rivera, *Practical TensorFlow.js*, https://doi.org/10.1007/978-1-4842-6273-3_9

follows *t*, a feature that serves to do forecasting and to generate sequences. This latest point makes RNN an excellent architecture for natural language processing applications. As we will soon see, RNNs can memorize order, making them suitable at identifying parts of a sentence, translation, and even generating creative content. For example, if you feed an RNN with a dataset made of lyrics of your favorite artist, it could learn how to create songs that follow the same pattern or style as the input data. Other RNN applications include identifying spam users using a sequence of events (Jugel et al., 2019), traffic forecasting (Zhao et al., 2017), and analyzing time series data, as we will do here.

In the first part of this chapter, we will go through the steps of creating and training two recurrent neural networks to do **time series forecasting** using the steps dataset introduced earlier in the book. The first RNN forecasts a single point in the future, while the second forecasts multiple steps. Then, we will create a second app that loads an ml5.js' RNN trained on a corpus of Shakespeare's works to **generate** "Shakespeare-like" texts.

Understanding RNN and LSTM

To understand the idea behind a sentence, you, the reader, must have understood the words that came before. Do you agree?

As we read, we inadvertently connect the meaning of the current word with the past ones to comprehend what the complete text says. In other words, the data we just read does not vanish from our heads—we preserve it. Recurrent neural networks do this too. Unlike other artificial neural networks, RNNs have the capability of persisting information inside them.

The networks we have used so far share the characteristic that the activations (tensors) flow in one direction: forward. For instance, in an epoch of a CNN training, the data flows from a convolutional layer to a max pooling layer. RNNs are not like this. Their basic unit, a recurrent neuron, has an input that connects back to the neuron, creating a loop in which the neuron sends outputs back to itself.

Figure 9-1 presents an example of a simple recurrent neuron, where x is the input and y the output. At each timestep t of the training, the node receives an input X^t (the sequence) and the output from the previous time step $t - 1$ (see the loop?) to produce a new output y^t. As a result, because of this iterative behavior, the neuron outputs become a function of the past ones. So, we could say that this function has an internal state (or memory) denoted by h and mathematically defined as $h^t = f(h^{(t-1)}, x^t)$.

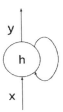

Figure 9-1. *A recurrent neuron*

Pop quiz time. Let me ask, do you remember the first sentence of this section? (Please say no because otherwise the example will not work). Right? I do not remember it either. It's been quite some time since we read it, and thus we forgot about it. Recurrent neural networks also experience this problem. The longer the sequence is, the harder it is for the network to remember what came first. Simply said, it becomes harder to keep "long-term dependencies" (Bengio et al., 1994).

To address this drawback, in 1997, *Sepp Hochreiter* and *Jürgen Schmidhuber* introduced an RNN architecture named "Long Short-Term Memory" or LSTM (Hochreiter & Schmidhuber, 1997). The details of the algorithm are well beyond the scope of the book. However, to get an idea, let's briefly review its principal feature. Simply said, an LSTM is a cell (we can also call it node) that remembers by keeping data within it. To regulate what information it preserves, that is, what is added and what is removed, it uses three units known as **gates**.

An LSTM cell has three gates: the *forget*, *input*, and *output* gates.
The forget gate decides what information gets discarded from the cell.
Conversely, the input gate controls what data enters the cell, and the
output gate decides whether the value in the cell is to be used when
calculating the unit's output.

For a complete explanation of LSTM and RNN, refer to the book *Deep
Learning* by Goodfellow et al.

About the data

The forecasting app uses a modified version of the steps' dataset used in
Chapter 1. This dataset contains the (normalized) number of steps I took
from July 9, 2019, to July 31, 2019, grouped in 15-minute intervals. Its shape
is [933, 61], where the first 60 columns are the steps taken at an arbitrary
timestep t, all the way to timestep $t + 59$, and each row is a sequence.
So, we have a sequence of 60 values. The last column is the target value
we want to forecast in the first RNN. For the second RNN, we will use a
different shape.

For context, Figure 9-2 illustrates the original dataset. On the x-axis is
the timestep t, and on the y-axis, the footsteps taken in that interval.

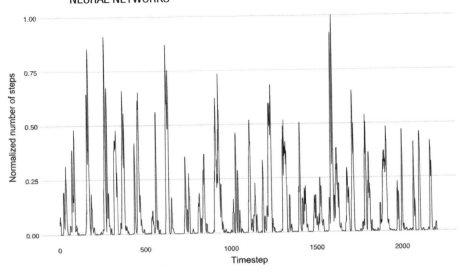

Figure 9-2. *The dataset*

Building RNNs for time series forecasting

The chapter's first application is a web app that trains an LSTM to forecast
the time step $t + 1$ of a sequence. This application, and the code, follows a
similar structure to those done in the first chapters of the book. It loads the
data, constructs the model, trains it, and visualizes the training stage using
tfjs-vis. To test the model, we will use a separate test dataset made of eight
testing cases. The testing involves visualizing the sample sequences, their
predicted value, and actual value. To create this plot, you will use Plotly.

Ready? Let's go. We will start by creating a directory, and inside it,
create a second one named "time-series." Then create the *index.html*,
index.js, and *style.css* files.

Preparing the app's interface

Figure 9-3 presents a screenshot of the app.

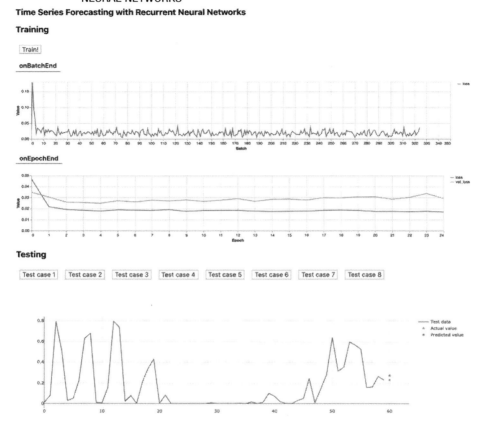

Figure 9-3. *The app. On the top part are the training visualizations
and at the lower part, the test cases*

It has a button that starts the training, a canvas holding the tfjs-vis
plots (no visor this time), the test case buttons, and the Plotly visualization
presenting the data. The following is the complete HTML:

```
<html>
<head>
  <script src="https://cdn.jsdelivr.net/npm/@tensorflow/
  tfjs"></script>
```

```html
<script src="https://cdn.jsdelivr.net/npm/@tensorflow/
tfjs-vis"></script>
<script src='https://cdn.plot.ly/plotly-latest.min.js'>
</script>
<link href="./style.css" rel="stylesheet">
</head>

<body>
  <div class="main-centered-container">
    <h2>Time Series Forecasting with Recurrent Neural
    Networks</h2>
    <h2>Training</h2>
    <button id="btn-train">Train!</button>
    <div id="canvas-training-tfvis"></div>
    <h2>Testing</h2>
    <div id='test-buttons'></div>
    <div id='plot'></div>
  </div>
  <script src="index.js" type="module"></script>
  </div>
</body>
</html>
```

First, we have the <head> node loading the required packages.
Following it is the body, made up of one large <div> with three <h2>
headers, the "Train!" button, the canvas for the tfjs-vis graphs, and the
divisions for the test buttons and the Plotly plot. At the bottom is the script
tag that loads the *index.js* script. Copy this code into *index.html*.

In the styling department, add the following CSS into *style.css*:

```
body {
  margin: 50px 0;
  padding: 0;
  font-family: -apple-system, BlinkMacSystemFont, "Segoe UI";
}

button {
  margin: 10px 10px;
  font-size: 100%;
}

.main-centered-container {
  padding-left: 60px;
  padding-right: 60px;
  margin: 0 auto;
  max-width: 1280px;
}
```

If you wish to see how it looks, start a local server using *http-server* on the project's directory and access the address provided. Once done, close *index.html* and prepare yourself to transform the dataset.

Transforming the dataset

Even though the dataset is already pre-processed, you need to do further work on it to transform it into a format compatible with the LSTM. As before, we will use the function tf.data.csv() to load the CSV dataset as a tf.data.Dataset object. But RNNs do not use this format. They require a tensor of rank 3 with shape (batch_size, timesteps, input_dim), where batch_size is the number of examples, timesteps the length of the sequence, and input_dim the number of features. In our case, with the dataset we have at hand, the batch size should be 933 (but let's use

900 since it is a nice round number), timesteps 60, and input_dim 1,
because we are only using one sequence feature (the number of steps). In
conclusion, the shape of the input tensor should be [900, 60, 1]. How do we
do this in code? Open *index.js* and follow me.

Start by defining the following variables at the top of the file:

```
const csvUrl = 'https://gist.githubusercontent.com/juandes/5c73
97a2b8844fbbbb2434011e9d9cc5/raw/9a849143a3e3cb80dfeef3b1b42597
cc5572f674/sequence.csv';

const testUrl = 'https://gist.githubusercontent.
com/juandes/950003d00bd16657228e4cdd268a312a/raw/
e5b5d052f95765d5bedfc6618e3c47c711d6816d/test.csv';

const TIMESTEPS = 60;
const TRAINING_DATASET_SIZE = 900;
const TEST_DATASET_SIZE = 8;

let model;
```

The first two are the paths to the training and test dataset. You can
either use the remote version of the datasets or the version located in the
book's repository (directory *9/time-series/data/*). Then come TIMESTEPS,
the datasets' sizes, and the model.

Next, create a function that loads both the training and test datasets:

```
function loadData() {
  const trainingDataset = tf.data.csv(csvUrl, {
    columnConfigs: {
      value: {
        isLabel: true,
      },
    },
  });
```

```
  const testDataset = tf.data.csv(testUrl, {
    columnConfigs: {
      value: {
        isLabel: true,
      },
    },
  });

  return { trainingDataset, testDataset };
}
```

Followed by a second one responsible for preparing the dataset:

```
async function prepareDataset(dataset, size) {
  const sequences = tf.buffer([size, TIMESTEPS, 1]);
  const targets = tf.buffer([size, 1]);

  let row = 0;
  await dataset.forEachAsync(({ xs, ys }) => {
    let column = 0;
    Object.values(xs).forEach((element) => {
      sequences.set(element, row, column, 0);
      column += 1;
    });
    targets.set(ys.value, row, 0);
    row += 1;
  });

  return { xs: sequences.toTensor(), ys: targets.toTensor() };
}
```

prepareDataset() has two parameters, dataset (a tf.data.
Dataset object) and size, the length of the dataset. It starts with calls
to tf.buffer() to create two TensorBuffers—a mutable object that
you can insert values to before converting it to a tensor—that you will

use to assign the sequence data to sequences (a rank 3 tensor) and the target values (what we want to predict) to targets (a rank 2 value). The function uses two loops to set the values in the buffers. The inner loop which iterates over each element of a single sequence (one row) sets these values to the sequence buffer, while the other one sets the target value. This method set() sets a value at a given location. In both cases, the last argument of set() is 0 because the last dimension of the buffer is of size 1. prepareDataset() returns an object where the key xs is the sequence tensor and ys the targets. And just like that, the LSTM is ready to accept the data!

Before proceeding to the next section, let's run the app and verify that it works. So, under prepareDataset(), create an init() function and call loadData() and prepareDataset() twice to prepare the training and test datasets. To double-check their shapes, use console.log(train.xs.shape), console.log(set.xs.shape). Their respective values should be [900, 60, 1] and [8, 60, 1]:

```
async function init() {
  const { trainingDataset, testDataset } = loadData();
  const train = await prepareDataset(trainingDataset,
  TRAINING_DATASET_SIZE);
  const test = await prepareDataset(testDataset,
  TEST_DATASET_SIZE);
  console.log(train.xs.shape);
  console.log(test.xs.shape);
}
```

Back at the browser, hit the refresh button to reload the app. Open the developer console and verify that the shape is the same as the one earlier.

Designing the model and training it

Time for the fun part (I know I keep saying that): creating the model. This forecasting model is a small recurrent neural network of one LSTM layer of 32 cells and a dense layer of one unit:

```
async function defineModel() {
  model = tf.sequential();
  model.add(tf.layers.lstm(
    {
      inputShape: [TIMESTEPS, 1],
      units: 32,
      returnSequences: false,
    },
  ));
  model.add(tf.layers.dense({ units: 1 }));
  model.compile({
    loss: 'meanSquaredError',
    optimizer: tf.train.adam(0.1),
  });
}
```

The preceding example is defineModel(), responsible for constructing and compiling the model. The initial line creates an instance of a Sequential model. Next are the layers, starting with the LSTM. Since it is the model's initial layer, it specifies the inputShape, whose value is the shape of the training dataset's last two dimensions. A second hyperparameter we need to define is units, which refers to the LSTM cells. The last attribute of the layer is returnSequences, a property of the RNN-related layers. This attribute specifies whether to return the last output of the sequence or the entire sequence. By default, its value is false, but for demonstration, let's explicitly define it.

Then, we compile. On this occasion, use the mean squared error loss function since the target output is a continuous variable. As for the optimizer, use Adam. Model finished!

On to the training. Under the previous function, create a new one named `trainModel()` with one parameter `trainingSet`. In the function, use `getElementById()` to get the canvas element that holds the tfjs-vis visualizations. After, call `model.fit()` using `trainingSet.xs` and `trainingSet.ys` as the first two arguments and a configuration object using the following attributes:

- batchSize = 64.

- epochs = 25.

- validationSplit = 0.1 to use 10% of the data to validate the training.

- As for the callbacks, use tfvis.show.fitCallbacks() to visualize the loss and validation loss values onEpochEnd and onBatchEnd.

```
async function trainModel(trainingSet) {
  const container = document.getElementById('canvas-
  training-tfvis');

  await model.fit(trainingSet.xs, trainingSet.ys, {
    batchSize: 64,
    epochs: 25,
    validationSplit: 0.1,
    callbacks: [
      tfvis.show.fitCallbacks(
        container,
```

```
      ['loss', 'val_loss'],
      { callbacks: ['onEpochEnd', 'onBatchEnd'] },
    )],
  });
}
```

Predicting and testing the model

By this point, you have loaded the data and created the model. So, the only missing step is implementing the testing functionality to assess its performance empirically. To test it, we will use a small dataset made of eight observations that do not appear in the training set. As displayed in Figure 9-3, the testing part of the application involves using one of eight buttons (one per testing case) to visualize the sequence and its predicted and actual values. With this approach, the user can visually assess how far the predictions are from the real value.

Developing this feature involves three different components, one for predicting, another for plotting the predictions, and another one for creating the buttons.

The first, predict(), is a function that uses model.predict() and returns its value. Instead of predicting each case individually, use the entire test dataset to obtain the eight predictions:

```
function predict(testingSet) {
  return model
    .predict(testingSet.xs)
    .dataSync();
}
```

The second function, named plotPrediction(), plots the predictions. It has three parameters, the test case's number, the test dataset, and the predictions array:

```javascript
async function plotPrediction(which, testingSet, predictions) {
  let testCase = (await testingSet.xs.array());
  testCase = testCase[which].flat();

  const traceSequence = {
    x: range(0, TIMESTEPS - 1, 1),
    y: testCase.slice(0, TIMESTEPS),
    mode: 'lines',
    type: 'scatter',
    name: 'Test data',
  };

  const traceActualValue = {
    x: [TIMESTEPS],
    y: [testCase[TIMESTEPS - 1]],
    mode: 'markers',
    type: 'scatter',
    name: 'Actual value',
    symbol: 'circle',
  };

  const tracePredictedValue = {
    x: [TIMESTEPS],
    y: [predictions[which]],
    mode: 'markers',
    type: 'scatter',
    name: 'Predicted value',
    symbol: 'diamond',
  };

  const traces = [traceSequence, traceActualValue,
  tracePredictedValue];
  Plotly.newPlot('plot', traces);
}
```

```
function range(min, max, steps) {
  return Array.from({ length: (max - min) / steps + 1 }, (_, i)
=> min + i * steps);
}
```

The first line of the function converts the values part of the test data (xs) to a nested array where each element is a test case. This test case array is also a nested one where each of the elements is another array. So, we need flat() to flatten it. After that, the same "range-like" function (defined after plotPrediction()) we used in Chapter 2 generates an array of values from 0 to 59 (the sequence length). Then comes the Plotly visualization.

For this visualization, you need three Plotly traces, one for the sequence, the predicted value, and the true value. But we also want the traces to look different. Therefore, we will specify their style. For instance, the sequence is represented with a line, and the other values with markers; feel free to customize it to your liking. After defining the traces, append them to the same array. Then call Plotly.newPlot() with the argument 'plot' (the id of the <div>) and the traces array.

Last, use the same createButton() from the earlier chapters to create the buttons:

```
function createButton(innerText, selector, id, listener,
disabled = false) {
  const btn = document.createElement('BUTTON');
  btn.innerText = innerText;
  btn.id = id;
  btn.disabled = disabled;

  btn.addEventListener('click', listener);
  document.querySelector(selector).appendChild(btn);
}
```

To put it all together, return to the init() function. There, use range()
to create an array and iterate over it to create the eight buttons and their
callback function that plot the prediction once clicked (which by default
are disabled). Following this, use once again getElementById() to get the
button that starts the training. Assign to it a "click" event listener that calls
defineModel(), trainModel(), and predict().

```js
async function init() {
  let predictions;
  const { trainingDataset, testDataset } = loadData();
  const train = await prepareDataset(trainingDataset,
  TRAINING_DATASET_SIZE);
  const test = await prepareDataset(testDataset,
  TEST_DATASET_SIZE);

  const testCasesIndex = range(1, 8, 1);

  testCasesIndex.forEach((testCase) => {
    createButton(`Test case ${testCase}`, '#test-buttons',
    `test-case-${testCase}`,
      async () => {
        plotPrediction(testCase - 1, test, predictions);
      }, true);
  });

  const trainButton = document.getElementById('btn-train');

  trainButton.addEventListener('click', async () => {
    await defineModel();
    await trainModel(train);
    predictions = predict(test);
```

```
    testCasesIndex.forEach((testCase) => {
      document.getElementById(`test-case-${testCase}`).
      disabled = false;
    });
  });
}
init();
```

Replace the old `init()` function with this one.

Running the app

Let's forecast. If the local web server is not up, please start it. Then
launch the application and click "Train!" to start the training. Below the
button, you will see two graphs displaying the *onBatchEnd* loss and the
onEpochEnd training and validation loss.

The average loss value (calculated after 10 tries) was around 0.02, and
the average training time 3 minutes long (on a MacBook Pro 2018). With the
training done, the eight testing buttons should be activated. Three of the
test cases (1, 2, and 4) have an actual value of 0, so the predictions should at
least be close to 0. In my tests, the outcomes of cases 3 (Figure 9-4),
6 (Figure 9-5), and 7 were very accurate, while case 8 showed the most
inaccurate result (the actual value is 0.90, and the predicted is 0.51).

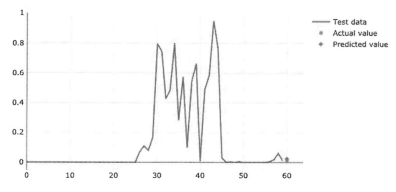

Figure 9-4. *Test case #3*

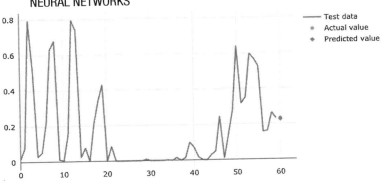

Figure 9-5. *Test case #6*

Multiple timestep forecasting

But wait a second? What about predicting a timestep $t + 2$? Is it possible?
Yes, it is. Forecasting only one step in the future is limiting and, honestly,
not that insightful. For example, you want a weather report that predicts
the complete trajectory of the hurricane and not just its position in the next
minute. Therefore, we will extend our forecasting model to predict the next
N future steps of the time series.

Extending the app implies two things: reshaping the data and, of
course, updating the model's architecture. As it is right now, our training
dataset's shape is [900, 60] and uses as target one of shape [900, 1]. But
we want to expand the target data to predict *N* values instead of 1. To do
so, we will vertically slice the training dataset to create a new one of size
[900, 60 - *N*] and a target tensor with shape [900, *N*]. For this example,
we will set *N*, now called FUTURE_TIMESTEPS, to 5 to predict the next five
steps. Let's start by creating the data (you can add the following code
snippets in the same file):

```
const FUTURE_TIMESTEPS = 55;
function prepareMultiDataset(trainingSet, testingSet) {
    let [xTrain, yTrain] = tf.split(trainingSet.xs, [FUTURE_
    TIMESTEPS, TIMESTEPS - FUTURE_TIMESTEPS], 1);
```

221

```
yTrain = yTrain.squeeze(2);
const [xTest, yTest] = tf.split(testingSet.xs, [FUTURE_
TIMESTEPS, TIMESTEPS - FUTURE_TIMESTEPS], 1);

return {
  xTrain, yTrain, xTest, yTest,
};
}
```

The function prepareMultiDataset() takes the training and test data
and slices them to create four: the new training and testing set and their
labels. yTrain requires tf.squeeze() to remove the last dimension ([900,
FUTURE_TIMESTEPS, 1] →[900, FUTURE_TIMESTEPS]).

Then comes the model training and designing function. Since our
problem is not as simple as the previous one, let's add an extra LSTM layer
to the model and set the returnSequences attribute of the first layer to
true. Unlike last time, we will call model.fit() from this function:

```
let multiModel;
async function trainMultiModel(xTrain, yTrain) {
  multiModel = tf.sequential();
  multiModel.add(tf.layers.lstm(
    {
      inputShape: xTrain.shape.slice(1),
      units: 16,
      returnSequences: true,
    },
  ));
```

```
multiModel.add(tf.layers.lstm(
  {
    units: 8,
    activation: 'relu',
  },
));
multiModel.add(tf.layers.dense({ units: yTrain.shape[1] }));
multiModel.compile({
  loss: 'meanSquaredError',
  optimizer: tf.train.adam(0.01),
});

await multiModel.fit(xTrain, yTrain, {
  batchSize: 32,
  epochs: 15,
  callbacks: [
    tfvis.show.fitCallbacks(
      document.getElementById('canvas-training-tfvis'),
      ['loss'],
      { callbacks: ['onEpochEnd', 'onBatchEnd'] },
    )],
});
}
```

We also need the function to perform the predictions. On this
occasion, we will use tf.Tensor.arraySync()—a method that converts a
tensor to a nested array—instead of tf.Tensor.dataSync(), because the
returned prediction tensor has the shape [8,5]:

```
function predictMultiModel(xTest) {
  return multiModel
    .predict(xTest).arraySync();
}
```

Next is the drawing function. Because now the app produces a
predicted sequence and not a single point, we need to change the traces to
draw lines instead of points:

```
async function plotMultiPrediction(which, xTest, yTest,
predictions) {
  let testCase = (await xTest.array());
  let targets = (await yTest.array());
  testCase = testCase[which].flat();
  targets = targets[which].flat();

  const traceSequence = {
    x: range(0, FUTURE_TIMESTEPS, 1),
    y: testCase,
    mode: 'lines',
    type: 'scatter',
    name: 'Test data',
    line: {
      width: 3,
    },
  };

  const traceActualValue = {
    x: range(FUTURE_TIMESTEPS, TIMESTEPS - 1, 1),
    y: targets,
    mode: 'lines',
    type: 'scatter',
    name: 'Actual value',
    line: {
      dash: 'dash',
      width: 3,
    },
  };
```

```
  const tracePredictedValue = {
    x: range(FUTURE_TIMESTEPS, TIMESTEPS - 1, 1),
    y: predictions[which],
    mode: 'lines',
    type: 'scatter',
    name: 'Predicted value',
    line: {
      dash: 'dashdot',
      width: 3,
    },
  };

  const traces = [traceSequence, traceActualValue,
  tracePredictedValue];
  Plotly.newPlot('plot', traces);
}
```

Last is the new *init* function, now named initMultiModel(), followed
by a call to it (make sure you comment out the previous call to "normal"
init()):

```
async function initMultiModel() {
  let predictions;
  const { trainingDataset, testDataset } = loadData();
  const trainingSet = await prepareDataset(trainingDataset,
  TRAINING_DATASET_SIZE);
  const testingSet = await prepareDataset(testDataset,
  TEST_DATASET_SIZE);

  const {
    xTrain, yTrain, xTest, yTest,
  } = prepareMultiDataset(trainingSet, testingSet);
```

```
const testCasesIndex = range(1, 8, 1);
testCasesIndex.forEach((testCase) => {
  createButton(`Test case ${testCase}`, '#test-buttons',
  `test-case-${testCase}`,
    async () => {
      plotMultiPrediction(testCase - 1, xTest, yTest,
      predictions);
    }, true);
});

const trainButton = document.getElementById('btn-train');
trainButton.addEventListener('click', async () => {
  await trainMultiModel(xTrain, yTrain);
  predictions = predictMultiModel(xTest);
  testCasesIndex.forEach((testCase) => {
    document.getElementById(`test-case-${testCase}`).
    disabled = false;
  });
});
}
initMultiModel();
```

Now refresh the app and start the training. This time, because we have
a larger model, the training is longer. Besides this, you will note that the
loss value barely changes (Figure 9-6); there is not a sudden drop like the
one before. It starts around 0.035 and converges at 0.025—not a significant
change. This behavior implies that there might be some problems with the
model. Let's see some test cases.

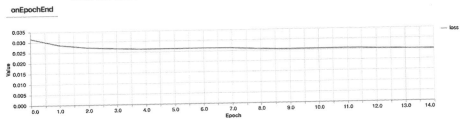

Figure 9-6. *The training's loss value*

Figure 9-7 shows test case #3. The solid line is the test data, the dashed line the actual value, and the dashed-dotted line the predicted one. Here, the prediction does not fit the actual data that well, but in overall, it follows the same pattern.

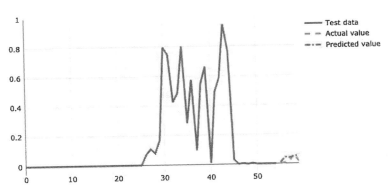

Figure 9-7. *Multimodel's test case #3*

But now it gets worse. Next is test case #6 (Figure 9-8), and its forecast resembles a *smoothed* form of the actual value—not a great outcome, but not an awful one.

Last, we have test case #8 (Figure 9-9), the worse of them. In this
example, the forecasted line trends downward, while the real value
increases.

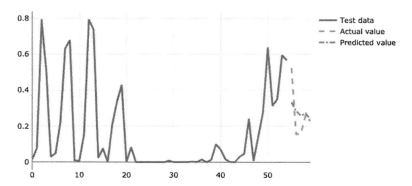

Figure 9-8. *Multimodel's test case #6*

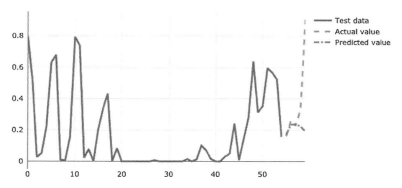

Figure 9-9. *Multimodel's test case #8*

From these examples, we could conclude that the model is not as
good as the first one—or at least not at predicting that far in the future. You
might have noticed that in most of the examples, the first three predicted
points were similar to the actual one, a sign that the model might be good
at predicting the near future, but not a far one. One of the exercises invites
you to try distinct FUTURE_TIMESTEPS.

It is sad to admit this, but sometimes a model does not work. The reasons could be many: not enough data, not the correct data, poor choice of a model, suboptimal hyperparameters, or a not suitable architecture. In this case, the dataset is very volatile and has many fluctuations, which might affect the training. Use this as a takeaway and a reminder that with all advances behind machine learning, it is not (yet) a perfect science.

But I refuse to end this section in such a low note. To experience a good multistep model, I will introduce a modified version of Jena weather dataset (Max Planck Institute for Biogeochemistry, n.d.). This dataset— typically used to showcase time series—contains weather information from the city of Jena, Germany, from the year 2009 to 2016. We will use the data to forecast the temperature. The dataset has the same structure as the previous one, so we do not need to modify the functionality of the program. But we need some small changes. To start with, we have to change the URLs of the training and test datasets to `https://raw.githubusercontent.com/Apress/Practical-TensorFlow.js/master/9/time-series/multiple-steps-jena/data/sequences.csv` and `https://raw.githubusercontent.com/Apress/Practical-TensorFlow.js/master/9/time-series/multiple-steps-jena/data/test.csv`. Alternatively, I would recommend getting the dataset from the repository because of its large size. You can find it at *9/time-series/multiple-steps-jena/data/*. Also, since the dataset is significantly larger, change `TRAINING_DATASET_SIZE` to 65000 and `FUTURE_TIMESTEPS` to 40, `batchSize` to 512, and epochs to 3. Then, launch the app and train as usual. But beware! A larger dataset implies having to wait longer to load the data and to train the model.

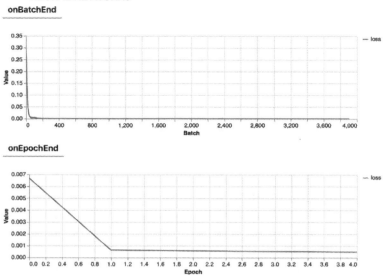

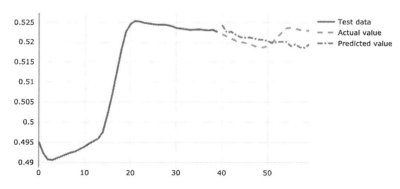

Figure 9-10. *Loss value during training*

Figure 9-10 presents the loss values after training the model for five epochs. The top chart, *onBatchEnd* shows that after just 50 batches, the loss drops to almost zero, while the second one, *onEpochEnd*, reveals that two epochs are enough. To see how the model performs, see Figures 9-11, 9-12, and 9-13.

Figure 9-11. *Test case #2*

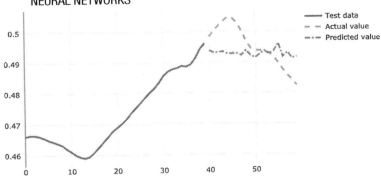

Figure 9-12. *Test case #4*

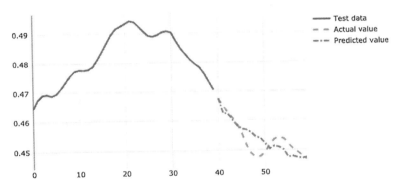

Figure 9-13. *Test case #5*

Way better than the last model. In all figures, the predicted forecast is very close to the actual one. If you look at the y-axis, you will see that the difference between the values is less than 0.01—a very accurate prediction.

Generating text using a pre-trained LSTM with ml5.js

A task where recurrent neural networks are great and shine at is text generation. If you look online or in the literature for RNNs' generative examples, you will be surprised by the number of unique, funny, and original applications people have developed. Some create lyrics, other musical chords, movie scripts, source code, and text that mirrors the writing style of classic authors of old, as we will do in this exercise.

Training these networks is not trivial. Behind them are an extensive architecture, an even larger training set, and a considerable amount of computational resources poured into it. As a result, we will skip the training on this one, not only because of the length or its complexity but also to have the chance of using a "battle-tested" model able to generate coherent text.

The model we will use is a pre-trained one provided by the ml5.js library. On its models' repository,[1] you can find several LSTM models trained on corpora containing the works of writers like *Shakespeare* and *Hemingway*. For this example, I will use the Shakespeare model. However, you can choose another one. The app itself is our simplest yet. Its purpose? Generating. The interface (Figure 9-14) consists of one text field used to write the model "seed," an initial piece of text from which the model generates its text. Also, there is an input slider that sets the prediction **temperature**, a value between 0 and 1 that controls the generated text "randomness." A low-temperature prediction gives a more "conservative" or confident output, while a high temperature produces more "creative" content (Karpathy, 2015).

---

[1]https://github.com/ml5js/ml5-data-and-models/tree/master/models/lstm

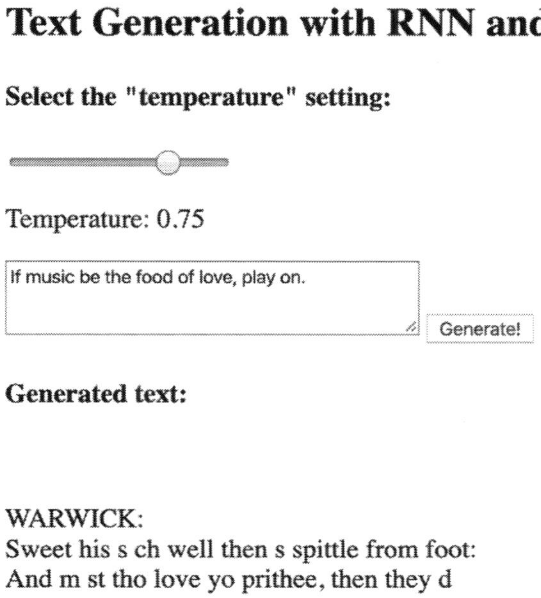

Text Generation with RNN and ml5.js

Select the "temperature" setting:

Temperature: 0.75

If music be the food of love, play on.   Generate!

Generated text:

WARWICK:
Sweet his s ch well then s spittle from foot:
And m st tho love yo prithee, then they d

Figure 9-14.   *A screenshot of the app. The box on top is the seed input,
and the text below, the generated text*

Developing the app

Start by cloning the ml5.js models' repository, available here: `https://
github.com/ml5js/ml5-data-and-models`. While it clones, create a
directory named *ml5js-text-generation*. When the download finishes, go to
the *models/lstm/* directory and copy the "shakespeare" directory to your
working directory. Then create the *index.html* and *index.js* files.

    Since the app code is minimal, I will present its entirety in this section,
starting with *index.html*:

```
<html>
<head>
  <script src="https://unpkg.com/ml5@0.4.3/dist/ml5.min.js"
  type="text/javascript"></script>
</head>
```

233

```
<body>
  <h2>Text Generation with RNN and ml5.js</h2>
  <div>
    <h4> Select the "temperature" setting: </h4>
    <input type="range" id="temp-range" min="0" max="1"
    value="0.75" step="0.25">
    <p>Temperature: <span id="temp-value"></span></p>
  </div>
  <textarea id="input" rows="3" cols="40" , placeholder="Enter
  the seed here..."></textarea>
  <button id="btn-input">Generate!</button>
  <h4>Generated text:</h4>
  <p id="p-output"></p>
  <script src="./index.js"></script>
</body>
</html>
```

The HTML's body has five main elements: a range for setting the
temperature, a `<p>` for displaying it, a `<textarea>` for defining the seed, a
button to predict, and another `<p>` to display the generated text. That's the
complete file—you may close it and open *index.js*.

In the first lines of *index.js*, declare a variable `model` and `temperature`:

```
let model;
let temperature;
```

After them, create the function `processInput()`. In the function, use
`getElementById()` to get the "predict" button and the output `<p>` element.
To the button, assign a click event listener that gets the seed from the text
area and uses it as one attribute of `model.generate()`, the method that
generates this text. Besides the seed, use the `temperature` attribute and
`length` to set the temperature and the desired length of the generated
sequence. This example uses a length of 100, but you may adjust it to your

liking. model.generate() has an optional callback that executes when the
model generates the sequence. Use it to assign the generated content to
the <textarea> element:

```
function processInput() {
  const btnInput = document.getElementById('btn-input');
  const pOutput = document.getElementById('p-output');

  btnInput.addEventListener('click', () => {
    const text = document.getElementById('input').value;
    model.generate({ seed: text, temperature, length: 100 },
    (_, generatedText) => {
      pOutput.innerText = generatedText.sample;
    });
  });
}
```

To get the slider's value, use the same updateSliders() function from
Chapter 7. In its callback, update the temperature value:

```
function updateSlider() {
  const slider = document.getElementById('temp-range');
  const tempValue = document.getElementById('temp-value');
  tempValue.innerHTML = slider.value;
  temperature = slider.value;

  slider.oninput = function onInputCb() {
    const val = this.value;
    tempValue.innerHTML = val;
    temperature = val;
  };
}
```

Last comes the `init()` function. Here, call `ml5.charRNN()` and use as its argument the path to the model and a callback that prints "Model loaded" once it loads. After this line, call `updateSlider()` and `processInput()`:

```
function init() {
  model = ml5.charRNN('models/shakespeare/',
    console.log('Model loaded'));
  updateSlider();
  processInput();
}

init();
```

With that, we conclude the app.

Testing the app

Let's generate classic literature. Like you, this is also my first time testing the model, so I am a bit excited. Before running the app, remember to start the local server on the project's location. Now run it. As a first example, I used as seed a classic Shakespeare quote, "all that glitters is not gold," and the default temperature of 0.75. The outcome was the following statement:

> *to s ch death,*
>
> *And so very heart they be this igland,*
>
> *In this wisdom, to tell p in his cast.*
>
> *VOL*

I do not know much about classic English literature, but I would say that it does sound very classic and dramatic (or at least the words I could discern from the text). But, overall, it is not a great text. It lacks

coherence, structure, and correct grammar. Granted that, it is a fun and
original line to read. But what if we lower the temperature to 0? See for
yourself:

> *With the windows with the people, and let him here,*
>
> *The command'd as the life and she shall be so s*

With a temperature of 0, the generated text corrects most of the
mistakes found in the last one. For instance, it resembles a complete
sentence, starts with a capital letter, and it even has a meaning. But is it
better? In some sense, yes. However, in my opinion, it is not as surprising
as the other. For other examples, see Table 9-1. I would suggest trying the
same seeds to discover how your results differ from mine. Last, if you wish
to have shorter or longer texts, change the length attribute. Enjoy!

Table 9-1. *Examples of generated text*

Seed	Temperature	Generated Text
To be, or not to be: that is the question	0.50	*of the* *bowls and the goodly seat of his hands.* *First Senator:* *Come, sir, then, good now yo have n*
A man can die but once	0.25	*That we m st be so well as the sea* *That the matter of the s n that hath dead* *I cannot s ppose the p*
Nothing will come of nothing	1.00	*That is lives to remons have sea and a idle not take* *Where I mine elsel that heaven, whence thirtle*

Recap and conclusion

An LSTM is a unique and versatile neural network architecture. It has loops, it remembers, and it generates. For example, with the right data, you could turn a model into a music producer or into one that foresees whether you will take a shower this morning. In this chapter, we experimented with four LSTMs for two tasks: time series forecasting and text generation. For the time series exercise, we created two LSTMs, one for predicting a single point in the future and another for predicting multiple steps. The first model performed satisfactorily. In our tests, we saw that many of its predicted values were near the actual one. Regarding the multiple-step model, the first one could somehow predict the general trend of the data, but not at a precise level, while the Jena model forecasted 20 steps in the future with high precision. For the second task, we used ml5.js and a pre-trained model to generate text that depicts the writing style of Shakespeare.

In the next chapter, we will continue with the theme of generative AI. But instead of text, we will create images.

EXERCISES

1. What is a recurrent neural network? What makes it unique?

2. What is the "long-term dependencies" problem?

3. What would be another suitable application where the input is a sequence and the output is a single value? Or a sequence-to-sequence example?

4. Another type of cell for RNN is the **Gated Recurrent Unit** (Cho
    et al., 2014) or GRU, a simpler cell that combined the forget
    and input gates into one structure, named update gate. In
    TensorFlow.js, you can add a GRU layer using `tf.layers.`
    `gru()`. Replace the LSTM with GRU and compare their
    performance.

5. Try different values of `FUTURE_TIMESTEPS` and re-train the
    multistep model.

6. Fit an LSTM with a dataset of your choice. A good place to start
    searching is `www.kaggle.com/tags/time-series`. I'd
    recommend starting with weather or stocks dataset.

CHAPTER 10

Generating handwritten digits with generative adversarial networks

In Chapter 9, we delved into the generative and creative side of deep learning. There, we used two recurrent neural networks to forecast and generate classical-looking passages of text. But text data, or generally speaking, sequential data, is not the only thing that these neural networks can create. Images are possible too.

If there is a recent and radical algorithm that has taken over the machine learning field, it has to be the **generative adversarial networks** (Goodfellow et al., 2014), or GANs. GANs—which *Yann LeCun*, one of the leading computer scientists in the field and corecipient of the Turing Award in 2018,[1] called "the most interesting idea in the last ten years in machine learning"—are a network architecture capable of creating incredibly realistic images that are almost indistinguishable from genuine

---

[1]Along with Yoshua Bengio and Geoffrey Hinton.

ones. Like RNNs, the applications and use cases of GANs are vast. For instance, GANs do **image-to-image translation** (Isola et al., 2017), the task of translating an image from domain X to Y, for example, converting a picture of a horse to a zebra. They can improve an image's resolution, a use case known as **super-resolution** (Ledig et al., 2017), and even replace someone's face for another one in an image or video, a technique called **deepfake**.

For the book's last exercise, we will build the "hello, world" of GANs, a GAN model that generates handwritten digits using the MNIST dataset as the source. Because of the long training time, we will run the training script using Node.js to get as much performance as possible. Then, we are going to write an app that loads the model and produce generated images. Our model's network architecture is based on the deep convolutional generative adversarial network (DCGAN) for the MNIST example[2] implemented with Keras (Python) Sequential API.

A friendly introduction to GANs

The central notion behind GANs is very intuitive. You have two neural networks competing against each other. One of them, the generator, tries to generate images that resemble the training dataset, while the second network tells if the generated image comes from the dataset or if it is generated. The system converges when the generator's synthetic images are so real that the discriminator can no longer tell them apart or, in simple words, once the generator fools the discriminator. Let's explain it with a simplified example.

The generator never sees an image from the dataset. Never. In our case, it means that it does not know how an MNIST digit looks like. Therefore, the first generated images are just random noise (Figure 10-1). Regardless

---

[2]https://tensorflow.org/tutorials/generative/dcgan

of this situation, the generator shows the image to the discriminator (the "judge"). But the discriminator knows how the dataset is, and upon seeing the generator image, it says: "You can't deceive me. I know how the dataset looks like, and this image looks nothing like it. I'm sure you created this." So, the generator, as training progresses, starts to assume how the real dataset looks like based on what the discriminator says and, therefore, begins to generate better images. Then, at some point, it shows one to the discriminator, and it says: "Oh, this image is perfect; I'm sure it comes from the dataset. I don't think this is yours." But, surprisingly enough, the image actually came from the generator. So, in the end, the generator fooled the discriminator, without ever, ever seeing an actual image from the dataset.

Figure 10-1. *An example of a generated image from an untrained generator*

Regarding the networks themselves, the generator is a neural network that produces images that mirror the target dataset. Its input is a vector of N random values (called the *latent space vector*) sampled from a random distribution (here known as the *latent space*), and the output is the image it wants to generate. So, its goal is to learn a function that maps the latent space into an image. The discriminator is a neural network that solves a classification problem. In our case, we have a convolutional neural network trained on fake data from the generator and real data from the training dataset. Its output is the likelihood of whether the image is real or fake.

Like CNNs, and, for example, MobileNet, there are GAN architectures specialized for specific applications. In our exercise, we will use the **DCGAN** (Radford et al., 2015) architecture, a class of GAN introduced in 2015 that proved to be more stable than the original GAN. This model uses a peculiar convolution technique to learn the features of the target images in an unsupervised manner.

Training a GAN

Let's do this (one last time). The model's training script consists of five functions:

- `makeGenerator()`: Defines the generator model.

- `makeDiscriminator()`: Defines the discriminator model.

- `buildCombinedModel()`: Builds a combined model made of the generator and discriminator.

- `trainDiscriminator()`: Trains the discriminator on a single batch of data.

- `trainCombined()`: Trains the combined model on a single batch of data.

We will dedicate one section per function.

After training the model, the next step is making a web app that uses the trained generator model to generate images and show them on the browser. As a side note, I should mention that the code you will see here ignores several of the ESLint rules we have been using throughout the book. This change aims to improve the code's readability—apologies for the lack of consistency.

Preparing the environment

Since we are using Node.js, first, we must define the package's manifest.
So, in the project's root directory, create a file named *package.json* and
paste the following JSON to it:

```
{
  "name": "tfjs-node-mnist-gan",
  "version": "0.0.1",
  "description": "Train a GAN for generating handwritten
digits",
  "scripts": {
    "train": "node trainer.js"
  },
  "dependencies": {
    "@tensorflow/tfjs-node": "^1.5.2"
  }
}
```

Then, execute npm i to install the dependencies.

Getting the data

As we did in Chapter 4, we will once again use a script from the official
TensorFlow.js examples repository to download the data.[3] But the script
differs from the one we used there. Instead of downloading the whole
dataset in one image, this one downloads four files that together complete

---

[3]The code was obtained from https://github.com/tensorflow/tfjs-examples/
blob/master/mnist-acgan/data.js. Parts of the script have been removed. Also,
the code is licensed under the Apache License. A copy of the license is available
in the appendix.

the dataset (a copy is available on the book's repository). Since the
chapter's primary goal is training the GAN, we will go through this code
without focusing so much on the details.

From the project's directory, create a new file named *data.js*. Then,
copy the following lines to import the modules and define several variables
related to the MNIST dataset:

```
const tf = require('@tensorflow/tfjs-node');
const fs = require('fs');
const https = require('https');
const util = require('util');
const zlib = require('zlib');

const readFile = util.promisify(fs.readFile);

const BASE_URL = 'https://storage.googleapis.com/cvdf-datasets/
mnist/';
const TRAIN_IMAGES_FILE = 'train-images-idx3-ubyte';
const TRAIN_LABELS_FILE = 'train-labels-idx1-ubyte';
const IMAGE_HEADER_BYTES = 16;
const IMAGE_HEIGHT = 28;
const IMAGE_WIDTH = 28;
const IMAGE_FLAT_SIZE = IMAGE_HEIGHT * IMAGE_WIDTH;
const LABEL_HEADER_BYTES = 8;
const LABEL_RECORD_BYTE = 1;
const LABEL_FLAT_SIZE = 10;
```

Next, define the fetchOnceAndSaveToDiskWithBuffer() function
to save the dataset to disk. If the file already exists, the function does not
download it again:

```
function fetchOnceAndSaveToDiskWithBuffer(filename) {
  return new Promise((resolve) => {
    const url = `${BASE_URL}${filename}.gz`;
```

```
    if (fs.existsSync(filename)) {
      resolve(readFile(filename));
      return;
    }
    const file = fs.createWriteStream(filename);
    https.get(url, (response) => {
      const unzip = zlib.createGunzip();
      response.pipe(unzip).pipe(file);
      unzip.on('end', () => {
        resolve(readFile(filename));
      });
    });
  });
}
```

The following function is loadImages(), responsible for calling
fetchOnceAndSaveToDiskWithBuffer() and loading the images:

```
async function loadImages(filename) {
  const buffer = await fetchOnceAndSaveToDiskWithBuffer
  (filename);

  const headerBytes = IMAGE_HEADER_BYTES;
  const recordBytes = IMAGE_HEIGHT * IMAGE_WIDTH;

  const images = [];
  let index = headerBytes;
  while (index < buffer.byteLength) {
    const array = new Float32Array(recordBytes);
    for (let i = 0; i < recordBytes; i++) {
```

```
    // Normalize the pixel values into the 0-1 interval, from
    // the original [-1, 1] interval.
    array[i] = (buffer.readUInt8(index++) - 127.5) / 127.5;
  }
  images.push(array);
}
return images;
}
```

Similar is the function loadLabels() that loads the dataset labels from a file:

```
async function loadLabels(filename) {
  const buffer = await fetchOnceAndSaveToDiskWithBuffer(filename);

  const headerBytes = LABEL_HEADER_BYTES;
  const recordBytes = LABEL_RECORD_BYTE;

  const labels = [];
  let index = headerBytes;
  while (index < buffer.byteLength) {
    const array = new Int32Array(recordBytes);
    for (let i = 0; i < recordBytes; i++) {
      array[i] = buffer.readUInt8(index++);
    }
    labels.push(array);
  }

  return labels;
}
```

Then comes the class MnistClass that handles the data. The class has a constructor that initializes this.dataset and the sizes of the dataset:

```
class MnistDataset {
  constructor() {
    this.dataset = null;
    this.trainSize = 0;
  }
}
```

MnistClass's first method is loadData(), a function that uses loadImages() and loadLabels() to read the data and labels. We will not need the labels; I decided to leave them in case you are interested in applying the script to another use case (this method and the next one go inside the class):

```
  async loadData() {
    this.dataset = await Promise.all([
      loadImages(TRAIN_IMAGES_FILE), loadLabels(TRAIN_LABELS_
      FILE),
    ]);
    this.trainSize = this.dataset[0].length;
  }
```

After loadData(), add getData(). This function converts the dataset into one large tensor and returns it:

```
  getData() {
    const imagesIndex = 0;
    const labelsIndex = 1;

    const size = this.dataset[imagesIndex].length;
```

```
const imagesShape = [size, IMAGE_HEIGHT, IMAGE_WIDTH, 1];
const images = new Float32Array(tf.util.
sizeFromShape(imagesShape));
const labels = new Int32Array(tf.util.sizeFromShape
([size, 1]));

let imageOffset = 0;
let labelOffset = 0;
for (let i = 0; i < size; ++i) {
  images.set(this.dataset[imagesIndex][i], imageOffset);
  labels.set(this.dataset[labelsIndex][i], labelOffset);
  imageOffset += IMAGE_FLAT_SIZE;
  labelOffset += 1;
}

return {
  images: tf.tensor4d(images, imagesShape),
  labels: tf.oneHot(tf.tensor1d(labels, 'int32'),
  LABEL_FLAT_SIZE).toFloat(),
};
}
```

Last, close the class, and add `module.exports = new` `MnistDataset();` at the end of the file.

Making the generator

Now let's make the GAN model, starting with the generator. Repeating what we discussed in the introduction, the generator takes as input a vector of random values sampled from a latent space and produces a tensor that represents the generated handwritten digit. So, throughout the training, the generator learns to project this vector to an image. Before getting to the model, create a new *trainer.js* file and add the following imports and constant variables:

```
const tf = require('@tensorflow/tfjs-node');
const data = require('./data');

const IMAGE_SIZE = 28;
const NUM_EPOCHS = 5;
const BATCH_SIZE = 100;
const LATENT_SIZE = 100;
```

The generator model consists of 11 layers (Figure 10-2). Layer number one is a dense layer with an input shape of 100 and output shape [12544]. The second one is a **batch normalization** layer. This layer normalizes the values of the activation tensor from the previous layer, meaning that it transforms its values to keep their mean near 0 and the standard deviation near 1. After normalizing comes a **leaky ReLU** activation layer, whose output is an activation tensor of shape [7, 7, 256]. Next, there is a transposed convolutional layer, which reduces the depth from 256 to 128. Following it is another batch normalization and leaky ReLU. Now it gets interesting. The next layer, another transposed convolution, is now used to *upsample* the width and height and reduce the width of the tensor. This layer "smartly" upsamples, meaning that it *learns* how to fill up the missing spaces during the upsampling operation. Last, we have another set of batch normalization, leaky ReLU, and transposed convolutional layer that transforms the tensor to [28, 28, 1], the size of an MNIST image. The following is the function makeGenerator() that defines the model:

```
function makeGenerator() {
  const model = tf.sequential();
```

```
model.add(tf.layers.dense({
  inputShape: [LATENT_SIZE],
  units: 7 * 7 * 256,
}));

model.add(tf.layers.batchNormalization());
model.add(tf.layers.leakyReLU());
model.add(tf.layers.reshape({ targetShape: [7, 7, 256] }));
model.add(tf.layers.conv2dTranspose({
  filters: 128,
  kernelSize: [5, 5],
  strides: 1,
  padding: 'same',
}));

model.add(tf.layers.batchNormalization());
model.add(tf.layers.leakyReLU());
model.add(tf.layers.conv2dTranspose({
  filters: 64,
  kernelSize: [5, 5],
  strides: 2,
  padding: 'same',
}));

model.add(tf.layers.batchNormalization());
model.add(tf.layers.leakyReLU());
model.add(tf.layers.conv2dTranspose({
  filters: 1,
  kernelSize: [5, 5],
  strides: 2,
```

```
  padding: 'same',
  activation: 'tanh',
}));

  return model;
}
```

Note   A leaky ReLU is another rectifier activation function like ReLU
that applies element-wise function $f(x) = 1$ if $x > 0$ or $f(x) = 0.01x$ to
the input tensor.

The newest hyperparameters we see here are the **padding** on the
transposed convolution and the **tanh** activation function. In Chapter 3,
we used convolutional layers with the default padding, "valid." This type
of padding ensures that the filter stays within the *valid* dimension of the
input (no padding is added), resulting in an output that is smaller than
the input, for example, if the stride length is 1, the width of the output is
(input) width - 1. In contrast, "same" padding guarantees that the output
size stays the *same*, as long as the stride length is 1. This is the reason why
the first two dimensions remain unchanged after the first transposed
convolutional layer. On the other hand, in a transposed convolutional
layer—which in some way is an inverse convolutional layer—a stride of
length 2 and "same" padding doubles the width and height dimensions,
hence the increase from [7, 7, ...] to [14, 14, ...] and [14, 14, ...] to [28, 28, ...]
after the second and third transposed layers. The activation function tanh,
short for the hyperbolic tangent, bounds the values to (-1, 1).

Layer (type)	Output shape	Param #
dense_Dense1 (Dense)	[null,12544]	1266944
batch_normalization_BatchNor	[null,12544]	50176
leaky_re_lu_LeakyReLU1 (Leak	[null,12544]	0
reshape_Reshape1 (Reshape)	[null,7,7,256]	0
conv2d_transpose_Conv2DTrans	[null,7,7,128]	819328
batch_normalization_BatchNor	[null,7,7,128]	512
leaky_re_lu_LeakyReLU2 (Leak	[null,7,7,128]	0
conv2d_transpose_Conv2DTrans	[null,14,14,64]	204864
batch_normalization_BatchNor	[null,14,14,64]	256
leaky_re_lu_LeakyReLU3 (Leak	[null,14,14,64]	0
conv2d_transpose_Conv2DTrans	[null,28,28,1]	1601

Total params: 2343681
Trainable params: 2318209
Non-trainable params: 25472

Figure 10-2. *The generator's layers*

Making the discriminator

Time for the discriminator, the soon-to-be-fooled model. This component
of the GAN is the judge, responsible for predicting whether the image
created by the generator comes from the real dataset or not—a binary
classification problem. We will define this model using a different method.
It will be more similar to how we did the transfer learning model, using a
tf.model() object to set the input and output.

Our discriminator has eight layers (Figure 10-3). It starts with a convolutional layer of input shape [28, 28, 1] and output shape [14, 14, 64]. After it is a leaky ReLU and a dropout layer. This combination of conv2D-leakyReLU-dropout is repeated once, producing a tensor of shape [7, 7, 128]. The tensor is then flattened to shape [6272] and sent through a dense layer with a sigmoid activation function. This last layer outputs a number between 0 and 1 that is the likelihood of the image being real or fake. The following is the function:

```
function makeDiscriminator() {
  let model = tf.sequential();

  // Hidden layers
  model.add(tf.layers.conv2d({
    inputShape: [28, 28, 1],
    filters: 64,
    kernelSize: [5, 5],
    strides: 2,
    padding: 'same',
  }));

  model.add(tf.layers.leakyReLU());
  model.add(tf.layers.dropout(0.3));
  model.add(tf.layers.conv2d({
    filters: 128,
    kernelSize: [5, 5],
    strides: 2,
    padding: 'same',
  }));

  model.add(tf.layers.leakyReLU());
  model.add(tf.layers.dropout(0.3));
  model.add(tf.layers.flatten());
  model.summary();
```

```
// Input and output layers
const inputLayer = tf.input({ shape: [IMAGE_SIZE, IMAGE_SIZE, 1] });
const features = model.apply(inputLayer);
const outputLayers = tf.layers.dense({ units: 1, activation:
'sigmoid' }).apply(features);

model = tf.model({ inputs: inputLayer, outputs:
outputLayers });
model.compile({
  optimizer: tf.train.adam(0.0002, 0.5),
  loss: 'binaryCrossentropy',
});

  return model;
}
```

Layer (type)	Output shape	Param #
conv2d_Conv2D1 (Conv2D)	[null,14,14,64]	1664
leaky_re_lu_LeakyReLU4 (Leak	[null,14,14,64]	0
dropout_Dropout1 (Dropout)	[null,14,14,64]	0
conv2d_Conv2D2 (Conv2D)	[null,7,7,128]	204928
leaky_re_lu_LeakyReLU5 (Leak	[null,7,7,128]	0
dropout_Dropout2 (Dropout)	[null,7,7,128]	0
flatten_Flatten1 (Flatten)	[null,6272]	0

Total params: 206592
Trainable params: 206592
Non-trainable params: 0

Figure 10-3. The discriminator's inner layers

The function starts by defining the hidden layers using various calls to
`model.add()`. These are the layers discussed in the previous paragraph. I
call them hidden ones because none of them are the input or the output.
Those are created separately.

After the last `model.add()`, there is a call to `tf.input()`, a function
that "instantiates an input to a model"[4] with attribute `shape` set to the
image's size. To add it to the model, we use `model.apply()`. To create
the output, we use the same method. First, define the dense output layer
and use the `apply()` to append it to the rest. With the input and output
layers specified, use `tf.model()` with attribute `inputs` set to `inputLayer`
and `outputs` to `outputLayers` to create the model. Then, compile it with
the binary cross-entropy loss function and the Adam optimizer with
`learningRate` 0.0002 and `beta1` 0.5, as specified in the DCGAN paper.
This second argument, known as an exponential decay, *decays*, that is,
reduces the learning rate over time.

Figure 10-4 presents the summary of the new model, where
`sequential_2` are the model's hidden layers.

---

[4]https://js.tensorflow.org/api/latest/#input

```
Layer (type)                Output shape            Param #
===============================================================
input1 (InputLayer)         [null,28,28,1]             0

sequential_2 (Sequential)   [null,6272]             206592

dense_Dense2 (Dense)        [null,1]                  6273
===============================================================
Total params: 212865
Trainable params: 212865
Non-trainable params: 0
```

Figure 10-4. *The discriminator*

Combining the models

Remember when we said that the algorithm trains both models simultaneously? That sentence was very literal. In this section, we will do something new: combining models. To be more precise, we will combine the generator and discriminator to create a new generator where the "original" generator comes before the discriminator (Figure 10-5). With the two models working as one, the output of the generator is directly used to update its weights after the discriminator classifies the generated image.

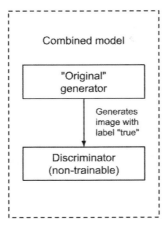

Figure 10-5. *The combined model*

In this combined version of the model, we will change the *trainable* property of the discriminator component to **false** so that the weights do not update while it is part of this new combined model. Hence, this part of the model does not learn; the discriminator (the one created earlier) learns separately in another function. While training the combined model, we will set the labels of the latent vector to 1 ("real") so that the discriminator believes the generated images are real. But we know they are not real. So, since the generator creates random noisy images (at first), the error rate early in training will be high, forcing it to get better.

This configuration can be very confusing, and so I want to repeat and clarify some details. First of all, we are still using the "original" discriminator—the one that learns to tell the pictures apart defined in the past section. Its role has not changed. But what about its weights? We just changed it to nontrainable. How is it still learning? Good question. But again, the discriminator **will learn** because we compiled it **before** making its weights nontrainable. With the combined model's discriminator, first,

we changed the trainable property to false and **then** compiled it, so it does
not learn. On the combined model, the discriminator's purpose is to assess
the generator performance on the "fake-labeled" generated images and to
produce the activation tensors needed to update the generator.

Let's see the function:

```
function buildCombinedModel(generator, discriminator) {
  const generatorInput = tf.input({ shape: [LATENT_SIZE] });
  const generatorLayers = generator.apply(generatorInput);

  // We want the combined model to only train the generator.
  discriminator.trainable = false;

  const discriminatorLayers = discriminator.apply
  (generatorLayers);

  const combined = tf.model({ inputs: generatorInput, outputs:
  discriminatorLayers });
  combined.compile({
    optimizer: tf.train.adam(0.0002, 0.5),
    loss: 'binaryCrossentropy',
  });
  return combined;
}
```

The model is built like the discriminator earlier. It uses a mix of tf.
input(), model.apply(), tf.model(), and the same compilation attributes
to form it. Note the discriminator.trainable = false line before
combined.compile().

Training the discriminator

With the models prepared, the next step is training them, starting with the discriminator and the function `trainDiscriminator()`. On this occasion, we will train differently. In the past chapters, we used `model.fit()`, a function that trains models "for a fixed number of epochs."[5] But our current situation is very different from the previous exercises. Now, we want to use the output of one model (the generated images) as the input of the discriminator. So, we need to have more manual control over the training. To train both models, we will use `tf.Sequential.trainOnBatch()`, a method that runs one training update on a single batch of data. With this function, we will be able to run one training update, generate images, use them as input for the discriminator, and run another training update. Later, we will design the training loop. But for now, let's see `trainDiscriminator()`:

```
async function trainDiscriminator(discriminator, generator,
xTrain, batchNumber) {
  const [samples, target] = tf.tidy(() => {
    const imageBatch = xTrain.slice(batchNumber * BATCH_SIZE,
    BATCH_SIZE);
    // tf.randomNormal is the latent space
    const latentVector = tf.randomNormal([BATCH_SIZE,
    LATENT_SIZE], -1, 1);

    const generatedImages = generator.predict([latentVector],
    { batchSize: BATCH_SIZE });
    // Mix of real and generated images
    const x = tf.concat([imageBatch, generatedImages], 0);
```

---

[5]https://js.tensorflow.org/api/latest#tf.Sequential.fit

```
  // The labels of the imageBatch is 1, and the labels of the
     generatedImages is 0
  const y = tf.tidy(
    () => tf.concat(
      [tf.ones([BATCH_SIZE, 1]), tf.zeros([BATCH_SIZE, 1])],
    ),
  );
  return [x, y];
});
```

```
const disLoss = await discriminator.trainOnBatch(samples,
target);
tf.dispose([samples, target]);
return disLoss;
}
```

trainDiscriminator() takes four parameters. The first two are the
discriminator and generator models, and the others are the training set
and the batch number. Inside the function is one large tf.tidy(), where
most of the functionalities occur. The first statement, xTrain.slice(),
creates a batch of images from the real dataset. Then, we produce the
latent vector (the noise) using tf.randomNormal(). The generator uses
this vector to create a batch of generated images (generatedImages). Next,
these images and the imageBatch are concatenated to form a tensor where
half of the data is real and the other half generated. After that, we build the
labels vector, where the vectors corresponding to the actual images are 1
(tf.ones()), and the labels of the generated images are 0 (tf.zeros()).
Outside of tf.tidy(), call model.trainOnBatch() using as arguments
the concatenated data and labels returned by tf.tidy() to execute one
training batch. In the end, return the loss value.

Training the combined model

Now the combined model:

```
async function trainCombined(combined) {
  const [latent, target] = tf.tidy(() => {
    const latentVector = tf.randomNormal([BATCH_SIZE, LATENT_
    SIZE], -1, 1);

    // We want the generator labels to be "true" as in not-fake
    // to fool the discriminator
    const trueLabel = tf.tidy(() => tf.ones([BATCH_SIZE, 1]));
    return [latentVector, trueLabel];
  });

  const genLoss = await combined.trainOnBatch(latent, target);
  tf.dispose([latent, target]);
  return genLoss;
}
```

The function is simpler than `trainDiscriminator()` because there is
only one model, and it does not require the real dataset. The only thing
needed is creating the latent vector and the labels, which, in this case,
are 1s because we want to trick the discriminator. Then, as before, use
`combined.trainOnBatch()`, and return the loss.

Putting it all together

After `trainCombined()`, create a new function and name it `init()`. Inside `init()`, call `makeGenerator()` and `makeDiscriminator()` and use their returned values as arguments to `buildCombinedModel()`. Next, use `data.loadData()` and `data.getTrainData()` to read the training set (we are not done yet with the function):

```
async function init() {
  const generator = makeGenerator();
  const discriminator = makeDiscriminator();
  const combined = buildCombinedModel(generator,
discriminator);

  await data.loadData();
  const { images: xTrain } = data.getData();
}
```

Now comes the training loop. All the past models we have trained use either `model.fitDataset()` or `model.fit()` to fit the model. With them, you simply specify the epochs and batch size, and it does the rest for you. Here, because of the multimodel characteristic of GANs, and because we are using `trainOnBatch()`, training with `model.fit()` is not possible. So, we have to define the training loop.

Repeating some definitions we saw in Chapter 2, the number of batches attribute describes the number of times the complete dataset passes through the network. Batches, on the other hand, is the number of samples a model sees before updating its weights. In code, this translates to creating one nested loop where the outer loop iterates `NUM_EPOCHS` time and the inner one, `numBatches` times. Then, at each iteration of the inner loop, we call the training functions (add this after `getData()`):

```
const numBatches = Math.ceil(xTrain.shape[0] / BATCH_SIZE);

for (let epoch = 0; epoch < NUM_EPOCHS; ++epoch) {
  for (let batch = 0; batch < numBatches; ++batch) {
    const disLoss = await trainDiscriminator(discriminator,
    generator, xTrain, batch);
    const genLoss = await trainCombined(combined);

    if (batch % 30 === 0) {
      console.log(
        `Epoch: ${epoch + 1}/${NUM_EPOCHS} Batch:
        ${batch + 1}/${numBatches} - `
        + `Dis. Loss: ${disLoss.toFixed(4)}, Gen. Loss:
        ${genLoss.toFixed(4)}`,
      );
    }
  }
}
```

Before the loop, we define numBatches, whose value is the length of the
training set divided by BATCH_SIZE. Then, we loop from 0 to NUM_EPOCHS,
and in the inner loop, from batch to numBatches. At each (inner) iteration,
call trainDiscriminator() and trainCombined(), followed by logging to
console the loss values every 30 batches. Last, after closing the loop, but
before closing init(), save the generator model using

```
await generator.save('file://model/')
  .then(() => console.log('Model saved'));
```

Then call init().

Testing the app

Is our model capable of generating images that resemble the MNIST dataset? Let's find out.

But before that, I would like to say a few words about the procedure. First, it takes time—a lot. With my setup, each epoch took around 12 minutes, so 30 epochs are 6 hours. You do not have to train for that long. Instead, I recommend starting small—manually evaluate the generated images (we will learn how now)—and keep increasing the number of epochs based on how good the model is. Likewise, you do not have to wait for the training to end to try the model. If you wish to test it while it trains, move the `generator.save()` line inside the outer loop to save a version of the model after each epoch.

While training, the program logs to the terminal the loss values of the discriminator and generator. Depending on the initial weights, these values might fluctuate a lot. This erratic behavior is (up to some level) acceptable. Keep in mind that a GAN is a fight between two models, and as one improves, the other worsens. During my tests, both losses were around 0.5 and 1.

Enough talk; let's do this. Back in the terminal, execute `npm run train` to start the script. Once the training ends, you can find the model in the *model* directory. To test it and see the generated images, return to the code editor, create a new *index.html* file and add the following code:

```
<html>
<head>
  <script src="https://cdn.jsdelivr.net/npm/@tensorflow/tfjs">
  </script>
</head>
```

```
<body>
  <canvas id="gen-img-canvas" width="28" height="28"></canvas>
  <button onclick="generate()">Generate!</button>
  <script>
    let generator;
    const realCanvas = document.getElementById('gen-img-
    canvas');

    async function generate() {
      const noise = tf.randomNormal([1, 100]);
      let generatedImage = generator.predict(noise).add(1).
      div(2);
      generatedImage = generatedImage.squeeze(0).squeeze(2);
      // If dtype is float32, it assumes the values are in
      // [0-1] range. If tensor is of rank 2, it draws
         grayscale.
      await tf.browser.toPixels(generatedImage, realCanvas);
    }

    async function init() {
      generator = await tf.loadLayersModel
      ('http://127.0.0.1:8080/model/model.json');
    }
    init()

  </script>
</body>
</html>
```

The preceding code is our generator app, an application consisting of one <canvas> and a <button> that, once clicked, generates an image using a function named generate(). Creating the generated picture follows a process like the one we used in the training loop. First, we must make a

latent vector and use it as the argument to model.predict() to output the
generated image. To draw the image on the screen, we have tf.browser.
toPixels(), a function that takes a tensor and displays it on a <canvas>.
Because we want to draw a grayscale image, the tensor must be of rank 2
and have its value between 0 and 1. But our tensor is not like that. Its rank
is 4, and the values are in the range [-1, 1] (remember the tanh activation
function?). So, we need to use tf.add() and tf.div() to bound the values
into the range [0, 1] and tf.squeeze() to remove the first and fourth
dimensions.

After generated(), add an init() function that calls tf.loadLayersModel()
to read the model from the given path. Last, to use the app, start a local
web server in the project's directory and launch it.

To illustrate how the generated images evolved, I will show several
images produced at different epochs. At epoch 1 (Figure 10-6), as expected,
it is just random noise. After 5 epochs (Figure 10-7), it is possible to notice
some basic shapes like curves and circles. On epoch 10 (Figure 10-8),
you can distinguish some digits like 9, and after 20 (Figure 10-9) and 30
(Figure 10-10) epochs, the model generates most complex numbers like 4,
5, and 6.

Figure 10-6. *Images generated after 1 epoch*

Figure 10-7. *Images generated after 5 epochs*

Figure 10-8. *Images generated after 10 epochs*

Figure 10-9. *Images generated after 20 epochs*

Figure 10-10. *Images generated after 30 epochs*

Recap

As Yann LeCun said, generative adversarial networks are indeed interesting and, if I may say, cool. Their ability to automatically create content has certainly earned them a spot as one of the most unique and revolutionary machine learning applications.

In this chapter, we successfully trained one to generate handwritten MNIST-like digits. But it was not an easy task. As fun as they are, GANs can be very complicated due to their simultaneous training property, the hyperparameters one needs to consider, the design of models' architecture, and of course how long it takes to train them.

You can find my generator model in the book's repository.

EXERCISES

1. What is a GAN? How would you explain it to a kid?

2. By looking at the models' architecture, could you tell which
   is the generator and which is the discriminator? What is their
   principal difference?

3. Run the training several times using different epochs. At what
   time did the images start to look like digits?

4. Use the MNIST classifier from Chapter 4 to identify the
   generated digits.

5. Train a DCGAN using one of the classes of the personalized
   dataset from Chapter 7.

6. Fit the model using the **fashion-MNIST** dataset (Xiao et al.,
   2017). This dataset serves as a drop-in replacement for the
   original MNIST dataset. The difference is that instead of digits, it
   has pieces of clothing. You can find it here: `https://github.`
   `com/zalandoresearch/fashion-mnist`.

CHAPTER 11

Things to remember, what's next for you, and final words

Welcome to the end of the ride. Through the last ten chapters, we have discovered, explored, and learned about the exciting field of machine learning with TensorFlow.js. With over ten unique examples that included a broad diversity of networks and use cases, we predicted the number of steps taken, clustered data, posed, identified toxic content, generated images, and more. It's been a lot.

It is for this reason that for the last chapter, I would like to close with a recap of some concepts we saw and even add more on them—we will call this section "Things to remember." Moreover, I also want to present a few pointers on how you could further extend what you learned here and offer some references that might help you in your future machine and deep learning adventures.

© Juan De Dios Santos Rivera 2020
J. Rivera, *Practical TensorFlow.js*, https://doi.org/10.1007/978-1-4842-6273-3_11

Things to remember

Tensors

This book was all about tensors and how they flow. So, it is very appropriate to start with them. As we learned, a tensor is a generalization of matrices of *N* dimensions with an attribute *rank*, *shape*, and *dtype*. Tensors have a very important property I want to highlight: they are **immutable**. Once their values are set, you cannot change them. So, every time we used a tensor method like `tf.add()`, we actually created a new one.

Another important fact about tensors is that we can change their shape. Functions like `tf.reshape()` (shown in the following) can turn, for example, a tensor of rank 1 into rank 2. Other functions that also modify a tensor's shape are `tf.squeeze()` and `tf.expandDims()`, to remove and add dimensions, respectively:[1]

```
> const tf = require('@tensorflow/tfjs-node');
> let x = tf.tensor1d([1, 2, 3, 4]);
> x = x.reshape([2, 2]);
> x.print();
> Tensor
    [[1, 2],
     [3, 4]]
> x = x.expandDims(2);
> x.shape
> [ 2, 2, 1 ]
> x.squeeze().shape
> [ 2, 2 ]
```

---

[1]To execute this (and some of the upcoming) code, launch Node.js interactive shell using $ `node` from a directory where tfjs-node is installed.

You can also perform mathematical operations on tensors. For example, on several occasions, we applied arithmetical functions such as `tf.add()` and `tf.div()` to add or divide the tensor's values by the given argument, for instance:

```
> const a = tf.tensor1d([1, 2, 3, 4]);
> a.add(2).print();
> Tensor
    [3, 4, 5, 6]
```

Similarly, it is possible to compute element-wise operations between two tensors:

```
> const b = tf.tensor1d([5, 6, 7, 8]);
> a.add(b).print();
Tensor
    [6, 8, 10, 12]
```

Last, we cannot forget about how to convert tensors to arrays. Functions like `tf.dataSync()` and `tf.arraySync()` return the tensor as an array or a nested array.

Memory management

Having many tensors takes a toll on your memory, causing unexpected slowdowns and, ultimately, crashes. That is why it is good practice to manage the memory of the application when working with extensive networks or when the app runs in the WebGL backend because it does not automatically garbage collect the unused tensors. To handle this problem, TensorFlow.js provides several functions to control the memory usage. Some of these are `tf.dispose()` to dispose of any tensor, `tf.tidy()` to clean up the tensors allocated within the given function, and `tf.memory()`

to return the program's memory information. One we did not use, but we ought to know, is tf.keep(), used to avoid disposing of a tensor created inside a tf.tidy():

```
> const tf = require('@tensorflow/tfjs-node');
> const y = tf.tidy(() => {
...    x = tf.keep(tf.tensor1d([1, 2, 3, 4]));
...
...    return x.add(1);
... });
> x.print();
Tensor
    [1, 2, 3, 4]
> y.print()
Tensor
    [2, 3, 4, 5]
```

But if you remove the tf.keep() function and try to use the tensor x, you will get a "Tensor is disposed" error.

TensorFlow.js Visualization (tfjs-vis)

A package we regularly used was **tfjs-vis**, short for TensorFlow.js Visualization. With the library, we frequently visualized the datasets we used and the training progress. But the library does more than this.

Other than drawing scatter plots, with tfjs-vis you can create bar charts (tfvis.render.barchart()), histograms (tfvis.render.histogram()), or line charts (tfvis.render.linechart()).

Besides visualizing data, you can also create more specialized graphs such as a prettier model summary (Figure 11-1) using

```
tfvis.show.modelSummary({ name: 'Model', tab: 'Summary'},
model);
```

Model			
Layer Name	**Output Shape**	**# Of Params**	**Trainable**
conv2d_Conv2D1	[batch,24,24,8]	208	true
max_pooling2d_MaxPooling2D1	[batch,12,12,8]	0	true
conv2d_Conv2D2	[batch,8,8,16]	3,216	true
max_pooling2d_MaxPooling2D2	[batch,4,4,16]	0	true
dropout_Dropout1	[batch,4,4,16]	0	true
flatten_Flatten1	[batch,256]	0	true
dense_Dense1	[batch,10]	2,570	true

Figure 11-1. *Model summary produced with tfjs-vis*

Or you can visualize the distribution of a tensor's values (Figure 11-2) with

```
const a = tf.tensor1d([1, 2, 3, 4, 5, 6, 6]);
const surface = {name: 'Values Distribution', tab: 'Tensor'};
await tfvis.show.valuesDistribution(surface, a);
```

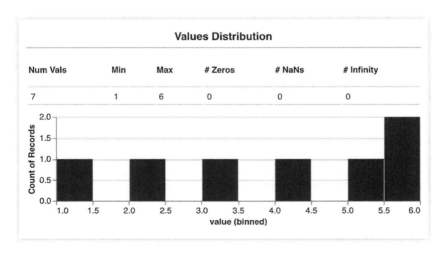

Figure 11-2. *Distribution of a tensor's values*

275

In the earlier chapters, we used tfjs-vis through its "visor" window. However, in Chapter 9, we learned that you could also present the visualizations on a `<canvas>` by using the canvas id as the first argument to the function:

```
const container = document.getElementById('canvas-training-
tfvis');
await tfvis.show.valuesDistribution(container, tensor);
```

For the complete reference guide, visit `https://js.tensorflow.org/api_vis/latest/`.

Designing a model

Designing a model is not a simple task. Creating one requires comprehending the dataset at hand, understanding every detail of the job one wishes to solve, and knowing the different types of layers available in the framework. This last point is not simple. If, at some point, you felt overwhelmed by the layers, and their peculiarities, let me assure you that that is completely fine. Over time, after designing many models, you will start to understand their differences and functionalities.

In TensorFlow.js, there are two principal ways of creating models. One is using the **Sequential** ("stack of pancakes") approach and the other, the **Functional** ("pancakes on the table") approach. Most of our exercises used the Sequential model, a model topology that describes a stack of layers where the output of one is the input of the next one. The Functional or `tf.model()` way is the graph-based alternative where you define the topology by specifying its input and output and connecting the layers using `tf.apply()`. Regardless of the type of layer, you must always declare the shape of the input tensor in the input layer. With a Sequential model, you can specify the shape using `inputShape` in the first layer. Or, if you are using a `tf.model()`, then you need to define the shape in `tf.input()`.

After designing the architecture, the next step is compiling and fitting the model. Before training a model, you always have to compile it to set the loss function, optimizer, and metrics attributes necessary for training. Then comes `model.fit()` to fit it. The parameters of `model.fit()` are the training data, the targets, or, in the case of `model.fitDataset()`, a `tf.data.Dataset` object. In both cases, you also need an object to configure the hyperparameters. Of these hyperparameters, you should at least define the batch size and number of epochs. Otherwise, the model will use the default values. Other important attributes are the callbacks, validation data, and shuffle.

For more information about the layers, visit the documentation at `https://js.tensorflow.org/api/latest/#Layers`.

Hyperparameters and attributes

If designing a network's architecture is complicated, deciding its hyperparameters' values is arguably even more. There is no right or wrong set of attributes for a network. After all, each dataset and use case is different. However, there are best practices and guidelines that serve as a starting point. Remember the DCGAN from Chapter 10? The learning rate of 0.0002 we used came from the paper that describes the model. My recommendation is that, when creating a model, check the literature, projects, or tutorials to find configurations that have worked for others. Try these configurations. Study how they influence the model's performance. Doing so will give you an idea of how to approach the problem.

Another essential attribute to consider is the loss function. Unlike hyperparameters, the loss function is directly bound to the model's task. So, choosing one is more straightforward than selecting, let's say, the number of epochs. For example, if the task at hand is a regression problem, the mean squared error is an optimal option. If the problem is classification, binary cross-entropy performs well for binary classification, just like categorical cross-entropy works for multiclass classification. Table 11-1 summarizes this information.

Table 11-1. *Loss functions suitable for certain tasks*

Task	Target	Loss Function	Last Layer's Activation Function
Regression	Continuous value	Mean squared error	-
Classification	Binary classification	Binary cross-entropy	Sigmoid
Classification	Multiclass classification	Categorical cross-entropy	Softmax

Testing

In software development, testing is essential, and yet, in the book, we did not perform any kind of test. The reason I omitted the test cases was to simplify the code as much as possible. But behind the scenes, I performed various tests that mostly involved confirming the shape of tensors or their values. To test statements in TensorFlow.js, the API provides a function, `tf.util.assert()`, that asserts if an expression is true. To illustrate it, consider the following example where we test the shape of a tensor:

```
> const tf = require('@tensorflow/tfjs-node');
> const a = tf.tensor2d([1, 2, 3, 4], [2, 2]);
> tf.util.assert(JSON.stringify(a.shape) == JSON.stringify([2, 2]),
  'shape is not [2,2]');
> tf.util.assert(JSON.stringify(a.shape) == JSON.stringify([2, 3]),
  'shape is not [2,3]');
Uncaught Error: shape is not [2,3]
    at Object.assert (/.../node_modules/@tensorflow/tfjs-core/
    dist/util.js:105:15)
```

In the first example, we are testing if the shape of the tensor a is [2, 2]. If true (like here), nothing happens. Note that for comparing the shapes (which are arrays), we had to convert them to strings and compare those. If the expression is not true (the second test case), it returns the message provided in the second argument. A second common testing scenario is asserting the range of a tensor's values, like this:

```
> const b = tf.tensor1d([-1, 0, 1]);
> tf.util.assert(
...    b.min().dataSync()[0] >= -1 && b.max().dataSync()[0] <= 1,
...    'values outside range',
... );
```

In this example, we used `tf.min()` and `tf.max()` to check if the values of the tensor are between -1 and 1, a scenario we saw in Chapter 10. The indexing is used because `dataSync()` returns the min or max value in an array of length 1.

Asynchronous code

While this point is not only related to TensorFlow.js, it is worth mentioning that when developing web applications, you should consider using asynchronous code to avoid blocking the app. Potential scenarios include calls to the functions `tf.Sequential.fitDataset()` and `tf.loadLayersModel()` or, in general, when executing a function that might cause a noticeable pause in the app. In our examples, we used the synchronous version—`tf.dataSync()` and `tf.arraySync()`—of the tensors-to-array functions since we were not dealing with large tensors and the response was immediate. However, if necessary, consider using the asynchronous variants `tf.data()` and `tf.array()`.

What's next for you?

So, you finished the book. Does that mean you are done learning deep learning? Never! Deep learning, and the discipline of data, is a vast field that grows with every passing day. Fortunately, the applications and lessons we learned served as preparation to get you started and start exploring on your own. If you ask me where you should start, I would recommend exploring several of the TensorFlow.js pre-trained models we did not see, for example, the body segmentation model and the speech command recognition. After them, you could study other deep learning and machine learning concepts like embeddings, autoencoders, image segmentation, attention-based models, and dimensionality reduction algorithms. Regarding the latter, you can find an implementation of t-Distributed Stochastic Neighbor Embedding (t-SNE) in the official TensorFlow.js repository.[2] However, at the time of writing, the library has not been updated to the latest version of TF.js. Another option is returning to the models we created to improve them. Add (or remove) more layers, use different data, tweak the hyperparameters, create a fun app, write a Chrome extension, and more.

If you want to take the models even further, try deploying them in other platforms, for example, mobile, cloud, or even on a desktop application using Electron. By deploying them somewhere else, not only will you get the chance to interact with them from a fresh perspective but also the opportunity of learning about a new framework. Additionally, try to experiment with TensorFlow (Python). Even better, once there, alter the models you already have (transfer learning, maybe?) to experience the similarity between the TensorFlow and TensorFlow.js frameworks.

---

[2]https://github.com/tensorflow/tfjs-tsne

And lastly, and above all, have fun. Train, deploy, make, break, visualize, design, question, and enjoy—that is, in my opinion, the best way of learning.

External resources

The following is a list of external resources to guide you through your TensorFlow.js adventures:

- The official API documentation at `https://js.tensorflow.org/api/latest/`: This is the library's guide. In it, you will find documentation about every single function and object TensorFlow.js has to offer.

- StackOverflow's TensorFlow.js tag at `https://stackoverflow.com/questions/tagged/tensorflow.js`: Use this tag to ask questions or find answers (now you should be able to answer some!).

- The TensorFlow.js' GitHub issues tab at `https://github.com/tensorflow/tfjs/issues`: This is mostly for reporting bugs and issues with the library, and not for asking help. Notwithstanding, you might find some answers here, especially when they are related to bugs.

- For finding datasets, try *Kaggle's Dataset* (`www.kaggle.com/datasets`) collection or *Google Dataset Search* (`https://datasetsearch.research.google.com/`).

- For the theory and mathematics behind the concepts here introduced, I highly recommend the book *Deep Learning* by Ian Goodfellow, Yoshua Bengio, and Aaron Courville.

- The topics we covered here belong mostly to the subfield of deep learning. But machine learning is more about networks and tensors. If you wish to learn more about machine learning in general, I recommend reading *Hands-on Scikit-Learn for Machine Learning Applications* by David Paper (Apress) and *Hands-On Machine Learning with Scikit-Learn, Keras & TensorFlow* by Aurélien Géron (O'Reilly).

Thank you

As cliché as it sounds, I want to end by saying thank you. This book has been not only a journey for you but for me, too. Every single line of code, concept, and piece of information you learned here was also a lesson for me. I am grateful for that.

As said in the beginning of this book, I wrote this book during my backpacking adventures. In fact, as I am writing this line, I am stuck in New Zealand in the middle of the Coronavirus crisis. So, behind every page you read, there is a new city, a different company, an exciting tale, or even a terrible Internet connection. But even though I was exposed to those changes, the only constant thing was the desire to bring a great book about TensorFlow.js and machine learning to you.

I truly hope that through the last 11 chapters, you have gained a whole world of knowledge that will follow you in your future endeavors. If you have questions, find an error, or want to show me your newest app, please contact me on Twitter: `https://twitter.com/jdiossantos`. I would love to hear from you.

Stay cool!

Juan :)

April 7, 2020, Christchurch, New Zealand

APPENDIX A

Apache License 2.0

Apache License
Version 2.0, January 2004
`http://www.apache.org/licenses/`

TERMS AND CONDITIONS FOR USE, REPRODUCTION, AND DISTRIBUTION

1. Definitions.

    "License" shall mean the terms and conditions for use, reproduction, and distribution as defined by Sections 1 through 9 of this document.

    "Licensor" shall mean the copyright owner or entity authorized by the copyright owner that is granting the License.

    "Legal Entity" shall mean the union of the acting entity and all other entities that control, are controlled by, or are under common control with that entity. For the purposes of this definition,

© Juan De Dios Santos Rivera 2020
J. Rivera, *Practical TensorFlow.js*, https://doi.org/10.1007/978-1-4842-6273-3

"control" means (i) the power, direct or indirect, to cause the direction or management of such entity, whether by contract or otherwise, or (ii) ownership of fifty percent (50%) or more of the outstanding shares, or (iii) beneficial ownership of such entity.

"You" (or "Your") shall mean an individual or Legal Entity exercising permissions granted by this License.

"Source" form shall mean the preferred form for making modifications, including but not limited to software source code, documentation source, and configuration files.

"Object" form shall mean any form resulting from mechanical transformation or translation of a Source form, including but not limited to compiled object code, generated documentation, and conversions to other media types.

"Work" shall mean the work of authorship, whether in Source or Object form, made available under the License, as indicated by a copyright notice that is included in or attached to the work (an example is provided in the Appendix below).

"Derivative Works" shall mean any work, whether in Source or Object form, that is based on (or derived from) the Work and for which the editorial revisions, annotations, elaborations, or other modifications represent, as a whole, an original work of authorship. For the purposes of this License, Derivative Works shall not include works that remain separable from, or merely link (or bind by name) to the interfaces of, the Work and Derivative Works thereof.

"Contribution" shall mean any work of authorship, including the original version of the Work and any modifications or additions to that Work or Derivative Works thereof, that is intentionally submitted to Licensor for inclusion in the Work by the copyright owner or by an individual or Legal Entity authorized to submit on behalf of the copyright owner. For the purposes of this definition, "submitted" means any form of electronic, verbal, or written communication sent to the Licensor or its representatives, including but not limited to communication on electronic mailing lists, source code control systems, and issue tracking systems that are managed by, or on behalf of, the Licensor for the purpose of discussing and improving the Work, but excluding communication that is conspicuously marked or otherwise designated in writing by the copyright owner as "Not a Contribution."

"Contributor" shall mean Licensor and any individual or Legal Entity on behalf of whom a Contribution has been received by Licensor and subsequently incorporated within the Work.

2. Grant of Copyright License. Subject to the terms and conditions of this License, each Contributor hereby grants to You a perpetual, worldwide, non-exclusive, no-charge, royalty-free, irrevocable copyright

license to reproduce, prepare Derivative Works of, publicly display, publicly perform, sublicense, and distribute the Work and such Derivative Works in Source or Object form.

3. Grant of Patent License. Subject to the terms and conditions of this License, each Contributor hereby grants to You a perpetual, worldwide, non-exclusive, no-charge, royalty-free, irrevocable (except as stated in this section) patent license to make, have made, use, offer to sell, sell, import, and otherwise transfer the Work, where such license applies only to those patent claims licensable by such Contributor that are necessarily infringed by their Contribution(s) alone or by combination of their Contribution(s) with the Work to which such Contribution(s) was submitted. If You institute patent litigation against any entity (including a cross-claim or counterclaim in a lawsuit) alleging that the Work or a Contribution incorporated within the Work constitutes direct or contributory patent infringement, then any patent licenses granted to You under this License for that Work shall terminate as of the date such litigation is filed.

4. Redistribution. You may reproduce and distribute copies of the Work or Derivative Works thereof in any medium, with or without modifications, and in Source or Object form, provided that You meet the following conditions:

(a) You must give any other recipients of the Work or Derivative Works a copy of this License; and

(b) You must cause any modified files to carry prominent notices stating that You changed the files; and

(c) You must retain, in the Source form of any Derivative Works that You distribute, all copyright, patent, trademark, and attribution notices from the Source form of the Work, excluding those notices that do not pertain to any part of the Derivative Works; and

(d) If the Work includes a "NOTICE" text file as part of its distribution, then any Derivative Works that You distribute must include a readable copy of the attribution notices contained within such NOTICE file, excluding those notices that do not pertain to any part of the Derivative Works, in at least one of the following places: within a NOTICE text file distributed as part of the Derivative Works; within the Source form or documentation, if provided along with the Derivative Works; or, within a display generated by the Derivative Works, if and wherever such third-party notices normally appear. The contents of the NOTICE file are for informational purposes only and do not modify the License. You may add Your own attribution notices within Derivative Works that You distribute, alongside or as an addendum to the NOTICE text from the Work, provided that such additional attribution notices cannot be construed as modifying the License.

You may add Your own copyright statement to Your modifications and may provide additional or different license terms and conditions for use, reproduction, or distribution of Your modifications, or for any such Derivative Works as a whole, provided Your use, reproduction, and distribution of the Work otherwise complies with the conditions stated in this License.

5. Submission of Contributions. Unless You explicitly state otherwise, any Contribution intentionally submitted for inclusion in the Work by You to the Licensor shall be under the terms and conditions of this License, without any additional terms or conditions. Notwithstanding the above, nothing herein shall supersede or modify the terms of any separate license agreement you may have executed with Licensor regarding such Contributions.

6. Trademarks. This License does not grant permission to use the trade names, trademarks, service marks, or product names of the Licensor, except as required for reasonable and customary use in describing the origin of the Work and reproducing the content of the NOTICE file.

7. Disclaimer of Warranty. Unless required by applicable law or agreed to in writing, Licensor provides the Work (and each Contributor provides its Contributions) on an "AS IS" BASIS, WITHOUT WARRANTIES OR CONDITIONS OF ANY KIND, either express or implied, including, without limitation, any warranties or conditions of TITLE,

NON-INFRINGEMENT, MERCHANTABILITY,
or FITNESS FOR A PARTICULAR PURPOSE. You
are solely responsible for determining the
appropriateness of using or redistributing the Work
and assume any risks associated with Your exercise
of permissions under this License.

8. Limitation of Liability. In no event and under no
    legal theory, whether in tort (including negligence),
    contract, or otherwise, unless required by applicable
    law (such as deliberate and grossly negligent acts) or
    agreed to in writing, shall any Contributor be liable
    to You for damages, including any direct, indirect,
    special, incidental, or consequential damages of any
    character arising as a result of this License or out of
    the use or inability to use the Work (including but
    not limited to damages for loss of goodwill, work
    stoppage, computer failure or malfunction, or any
    and all other commercial damages or losses), even if
    such Contributor has been advised of the possibility
    of such damages.

9. Accepting Warranty or Additional Liability. While
    redistributing the Work or Derivative Works thereof,
    You may choose to offer, and charge a fee for,
    acceptance of support, warranty, indemnity, or
    other liability obligations and/or rights consistent
    with this License. However, in accepting such
    obligations, You may act only on Your own behalf
    and on Your sole responsibility, not on behalf of
    any other Contributor, and only if You agree to

indemnify, defend, and hold each Contributor harmless for any liability incurred by, or claims asserted against, such Contributor by reason of your accepting any such warranty or additional liability.

END OF TERMS AND CONDITIONS

APPENDIX: How to apply the Apache License to your work

To apply the Apache License to your work, attach the following boilerplate notice, with the fields enclosed by brackets "[]" replaced with your own identifying information. (Don't include the brackets!) The text should be enclosed in the appropriate comment syntax for the file format. We also recommend that a file or class name and description of purpose be included on the same "printed page" as the copyright notice for easier identification within third-party archives.

Copyright [yyyy] [name of copyright owner]

Licensed under the Apache License, Version 2.0 (the "License"); you may not use this file except in compliance with the License. You may obtain a copy of the License at http://www.apache.org/licenses/LICENSE-2.0

Unless required by applicable law or agreed to in writing, software distributed under the License is distributed on an "AS IS" BASIS, WITHOUT WARRANTIES OR CONDITIONS OF ANY KIND, either express or implied. See the License for the specific language governing permissions and limitations under the License.

References

Abdel-Hamid, O., Mohamed, A., Jiang, H., Deng, L., Penn, G., & Yu, D. (2014). Convolutional neural networks for speech recognition. *IEEE/ACM Transactions on Audio, Speech, and Language Processing, 22*(10), 1533–1545.

Bengio, Y., Simard, P., & Frasconi, P. (1994). Learning long-term dependencies with gradient descent is difficult. *IEEE Transactions on Neural Networks, 5*(2), 157–166.

Borkan, D., Dixon, L., Sorensen, J., Thain, N., & Vasserman, L. (2019). Nuanced metrics for measuring unintended bias with real data for text classification. *CoRR, abs/1903.04561.* http://arxiv.org/abs/1903.04561

Cer, D., Yang, Y., Kong, S., Hua, N., Limtiaco, N., John, R. St., Constant, N., Guajardo-Cespedes, M., Yuan, S., Tar, C., Sung, Y.-H., Strope, B., & Kurzweil, R. (2018). Universal sentence encoder. *CoRR, abs/1803.11175.* http://arxiv.org/abs/1803.11175

Cho, K., van Merrienboer, B., Gülçehre, Ç., Bougares, F., Schwenk, H., & Bengio, Y. (2014). Learning phrase representations using RNN encoder-decoder for statistical machine translation. *CoRR, abs/1406.1078.* http://arxiv.org/abs/1406.1078

Conversation AI. (2018, December 10). *Annotation instructions for Toxicity with sub-attributes.* https://github.com/conversationai/conversationai.github.io/blob/master/crowdsourcing_annotation_schemes/toxicity_with_subattributes.md

Domingos, P. (2015). *The master algorithm: How the quest for the ultimate learning machine will remake our world.* Basic Books.

Gareth, J., Witten, D., Hastie, T., & Tibshirani, R. (2013). *An Introduction to Statistical Learning with Applications in R.* Springer.

© Juan De Dios Santos Rivera 2020
J. Rivera, *Practical TensorFlow.js*, https://doi.org/10.1007/978-1-4842-6273-3

Géron, A. (2019). *Hands-on machine learning with scikit-learn, keras, and TensorFlow: Concepts, tools, and techniques to build intelligent systems.* O'Reilly Media.

GitHub. (2019). *The State of the Octoverse.* https://octoverse. github.com/

Goodfellow, I., Bengio, Y., & Courville, A. (2016). *Deep learning.* MIT Press.

Goodfellow, I., Pouget-Abadie, J., Mirza, M., Xu, B., Warde-Farley, D., Ozair, S., Courville, A., & Bengio, Y. (2014). Generative adversarial nets. In Z. Ghahramani, M. Welling, C. Cortes, N. D. Lawrence, & K. Q. Weinberger (Eds.), *Advances in neural information processing systems 27* (pp. 2672–2680). Curran Associates, Inc. http://papers.nips.cc/paper/5423-generative-adversarial-nets.pdf

Google. (n.d.). *AutoML Vision documentation.* Retrieved April 18, 2020, from https://cloud.google.com/vision/automl/docs

Google. (2018a). *Models and layers.* TensorFlow. www.tensorflow.org/js/guide/models_and_layers#creating_models_with_the_core_api

Google. (2018b). *Tensors and operations.* TensorFlow. www.tensorflow.org/js/guide/tensors_operations

Google. (2018c). *Training models.* TensorFlow. www.tensorflow.org/js/guide/train_models

He, K., Zhang, X., Ren, S., & Sun, J. (2015). Deep residual learning for image recognition. *CoRR, abs/1512.03385.* http://arxiv.org/abs/1512.03385

Henderson, H. V., & Velleman, P. F. (1981). Building multiple regression models interactively. *Biometrics, 37*(2), 391–411.

Hochreiter, S., & Schmidhuber, J. (1997). Long short-term memory. *Neural Computation, 9*(8), 1735–1780.

Howard, A. G., Zhu, M., Chen, B., Kalenichenko, D., Wang, W., Weyand, T., Andreetto, M., & Adam, H. (2017). MobileNets: Efficient convolutional neural networks for mobile vision applications. *CoRR, abs/1704.04861.* http://arxiv.org/abs/1704.04861

Isola, P., Zhu, J., Zhou, T., & Efros, A. A. (2017). Image-to-image translation with conditional adversarial networks. *2017 IEEE Conference on Computer Vision and Pattern Recognition (CVPR)*, 5967–5976.

Jugel, U., De Dios Santos, J., Trautmann, E., & Behrens, D. (2019). Fighting spam in dating apps. In T. Grust, F. Naumann, A. Böhm, W. Lehner, T. Härder, E. Rahm, A. Heuer, M. Klettke, & H. Meyer (Eds.), *BTW 2019* (pp. 361–373). Gesellschaft für Informatik, Bonn. https://doi.org/10.18420/btw2019-22

Karpathy, A. (2015). *The unreasonable effectiveness of recurrent neural networks*. http://karpathy.github.io/2015/05/21/rnn-effectiveness/

Kingma, D. P., & Ba, J. (2014). *Adam: A method for stochastic optimization*. http://arxiv.org/abs/1412.6980

Krizhevsky, A., Sutskever, I., & Hinton, G. E. (2012). ImageNet classification with deep convolutional neural networks. In F. Pereira, C. J. C. Burges, L. Bottou, & K. Q. Weinberger (Eds.), *Advances in neural information processing systems 25* (pp. 1097–1105). Curran Associates, Inc. http://papers.nips.cc/paper/4824-imagenet-classification-with-deep-convolutional-neural-networks.pdf

LeCun, Y., Boser, B., Denker, J. S., Henderson, D., Howard, R. E., Hubbard, W., & Jackel, L. D. (1989). Backpropagation applied to handwritten zip code recognition. *Neural Computation, 1*(4), 541–551. https://doi.org/10.1162/neco.1989.1.4.541

LeCun, Yann, Bengio, Y., & Hinton, G. (2015). Deep learning. *Nature, 521*(7553), 436–444. https://doi.org/10.1038/nature14539

LeCun, Yann, Bottou, L., Bengio, Y., & Haffner, P. (1998). Gradient-based learning applied to document recognition. *Proceedings of the IEEE*, 2278–2324.

LeCun, Yann, Cortes, C., & Burges, C. (2010). MNIST handwritten digit database. *ATT Labs [Online]*. Available: http://yann.lecun.com/exdb/mnist, 2.

Ledig, C., Theis, L., Huszar, F., Caballero, J., Cunningham, A., Acosta, A., Aitken, A., Tejani, A., Totz, J., Wang, Z., & Shi, W. (2017, July). Photo-realistic single image super-resolution using a generative adversarial network. *The IEEE Conference on Computer Vision and Pattern Recognition (CVPR).*

LeNail, A. (2019). NN-SVG: Publication-ready neural network architecture schematics. *Journal of Open Source Software, 4*(33), 747. https://doi.org/10.21105/joss.00747

Lin, T.-Y., Maire, M., Belongie, S. J., Bourdev, L. D., Girshick, R. B., Hays, J., Perona, P., Ramanan, D., Dollár, P., & Zitnick, C. L. (2014). Microsoft COCO: Common objects in context. *CoRR, abs/1405.0312.* http://arxiv.org/abs/1405.0312

Liu, F. T., Ting, K. M., & Zhou, Z.-H. (2008). Isolation forest. *2008 Eighth IEEE International Conference on Data Mining,* 413–422.

Max Planck Institute for Biogeochemistry. (n.d.). *Max Planck Institute for Biogeochemistry, Jena weather data.* Max Planck Institute for Biogeochemistry. www.bgc-jena.mpg.de/wetter/

Murphy, K. P. (2013). *Machine learning: A probabilistic perspective.* MIT Press. www.amazon.com/Machine-Learning-Probabilistic-Perspective-Computation/dp/0262018020/ref=sr_1_2?ie=UTF8&qid=1336857747&sr=8-2

Oved, D. (2018, May 8). Real-time Human Pose Estimation in the Browser with TensorFlow.js. *TensorFlow Blog.* https://medium.com/tensorflow/real-time-human-pose-estimation-in-the-browser-with-tensorflow-js-7dd0bc881cd5

Papandreou, G., Zhu, T., Kanazawa, N., Toshev, A., Tompson, J., Bregler, C., & Murphy, K. P. (2017). Towards accurate multi-person pose estimation in the wild. *CoRR, abs/1701.01779.* http://arxiv.org/abs/1701.01779

Radford, A., Metz, L., & Chintala, S. (2015). *Unsupervised representation learning with deep convolutional generative adversarial networks.* http://arxiv.org/abs/1511.06434

Rosenblatt, F. (1958). The perceptron: A probabilistic model for information storage and organization in the brain. *Psychological Review, 65*(6), 386.

Rumelhart, D. E., Hinton, G. E., & Williams, R. J. (1985). *Learning internal representations by error propagation*. California Univ San Diego La Jolla Inst for Cognitive Science.

Russakovsky, O., Deng, J., Su, H., Krause, J., Satheesh, S., Ma, S., Huang, Z., Karpathy, A., Khosla, A., Bernstein, M., Berg, A. C., & Fei-Fei, L. (2015). ImageNet large scale visual recognition challenge. *International Journal of Computer Vision (IJCV)*, *115*(3), 211–252. https://doi.org/10.1007/s11263-015-0816-y

Shoeybi, M., Patwary, Md. M. A., Puri, R., LeGresley, P., Casper, J., & Catanzaro, B. (2019). *Megatron-lm: Training multi-billion parameter language models using GPU model parallelism*.

Srivastava, N., Hinton, G., Krizhevsky, A., Sutskever, I., & Salakhutdinov, R. (2014). Dropout: A simple way to prevent neural networks from overfitting. *Journal of Machine Learning Research, 15*(1), 1929–1958.

StackOverflow. (2019). *Developer Survey Results*. StackOverflow. https://insights.stackoverflow.com/survey/2019

Wan, L., Zeiler, M., Zhang, S., Cun, Y. L., & Fergus, R. (2013). Regularization of neural networks using DropConnect. In S. Dasgupta & D. McAllester (Eds.), *Proceedings of the 30th international conference on machine learning* (Vol. 28, pp. 1058–1066). PMLR. http://proceedings.mlr.press/v28/wan13.html

Xiao, H., Rasul, K., & Vollgraf, R. (2017, August 28). *Fashion-mnist: A novel image dataset for benchmarking machine learning algorithms*.

Zhao, Z., Chen, W., Wu, X., Chen, P. C. Y., & Liu, J. (2017). LSTM network: A deep learning approach for short-term traffic forecast. *IET Intelligent Transport Systems, 11*(2), 68–75.

Index

A, B

Apache License
    Accepting Warranty, 289
    to apply, 290
    contribution, 285
    derivative Works, 284
    disclaimer of Warranty, 288
    Grant of Copyright License, 285
    Grant of Patent License, 286
    Legal Entity, 283
    license, 283
    limitation of Liability, 289
    object, 284
    redistribution, 286
    submission of contributions, 288
    trademarks, 288

C

Clustering technique, 78
Convolutional neural
    network (CNN), 91
    convolutional layer, 92
    MNIST dataset app creation, 97
        canvas event listeners, 115
        categorical cross-entropy, 110
        CSS class, 98
        constructor, 101

createButton() function, 118
data.js file, 99
defineModel() function,
    107, 120
drawData() function, 118
dropout layer, 108
enableButtons() function, 119
flatten layer, 109
index.html file, 98
metrics model, 121
ModelFitConfig object, 113
model layers, 106
model.predict() function, 116
model.summary()
    function, 110
nextBatch() function, 103
nextTestBatch() function, 104
nextTrainBatch()
    function, 104
prepareCanvas()
    function, 114, 120
rectified linear unit., 107
softmax activation, 109
tf.memory() function, 112
tf.Sequential.fitDataset()
    function, 112
tfvis.show.fitCallbacks()
    function, 113

© Juan De Dios Santos Rivera 2020
J. Rivera, *Practical TensorFlow.js*, https://doi.org/10.1007/978-1-4842-6273-3

Convolutional neural
network (CNN) (*cont.*)
training model, 110
pooling layer, 95
stride, 93
PoseNet (*see* PoseNet)
createButton(), 120

D, E, F

Directory structure, 173

G, H, I, J

Generative adversarial networks
(GANs), 241
buildCombinedModel()
function, 264
combined model., 259, 260
deepfake, 242
discriminator, 254, 258
generator model, 250
batch normalization
layer, 251
layers, 254
leaky ReLU activation
layer, 251
tanh activation function, 253
image-to-image translation, 242
MNIST dataset, 242
data.js., 246
fetchOnceAndSaveToDisk
WithBuffer() function, 246
getData() function, 249

loadData() function, 249
loadImages() function, 247
loadLabels() function, 248
last model.add() function, 257
N random values, 243
numBatches, 265
package.json file, 245
testing, 266, 268, 269
trainCombined() function,
263, 264
trainDiscriminator() function,
261, 262
training model, 244
trainOnBatch() function, 264
Google Cloud account
cloud vision api, 167
dataset creation, 168
enable API, 168
evaluation tab, 170
exporting model, 172
labeling and annotating
images, 169
training, 170

K

k-means model, ml5.js library
app creation, 79
createClusterButton()
function, 84
index.html file, 80, 82, 83
Plotly graph, 87
testing model, 87
training function, 83

visualizeResult() function, 85, 86
clustering algorithm, 78
dataset, 79
overview, 79

L

Linear regression model
app creation, 57
Adam optimizer, 64
createLoadPlotButton() function, 62, 67
createPredictionInput() function, 70
defineAndTrainModel() function, 63, 66, 72
drawFittedLine() function, 69
fitted line, 70
forEachAsync() method, 60, 61
HTML file, 58
init() function, 63, 67
loadData() function, 60
loss and error values, 69
metric score, 65
model.fitDataset() function, 65
model.summary() method, 73
MSE loss function, 64
testing, 70
tf.data.csv() function, 62
training set, 70
using tfjs-vis, 60

workspace setup, 57
bad regression, 56
data overview, 56
overview, 54
Pidgey's HP and CP, 55
loadVideo() function, 176
Logistic regression model, 26
app creation, 33
activation function, 44, 45
batch() function, 48
compile() method, 46
createVisualizeButton() function, 42
CSVConfig object, 38
defineAndTrainModel() function, 50
dense layer, 44
document.
getElementById(), 50
document.querySelector() function, 43
evaluation metric, 46
forEachAsync() function, 40
HTML file, 33, 36
input shape, 45
loading dataset, 37
loss function, 46
loss and accuracy values, 52
model.fitDataset() function, 48
model.predict() method, 53
onEpochEnd callback, 49
onTrainEnd callback, 49
optimizer, 46
setting up workspace, 33

Logistic regression model (*cont.*)
    shuffle() function, 48
    tfvis.render.scatterplot()
        function, 41
    tfvis.show.fitCallbacks()
        function, 49
    units, 45
    visualizeDataset()
        function, 39, 43
    artificial neural network, 29
    artificial neural network, 31
    backpropagation, 32
    binary logistic regression
        model, 27
    data overview, 32
    discrete dependent variable, 27
    epochs, 32
    independent variables, 27
    perceptron, 29
Long Short-Term Memory (LSTM),
        ml5.js model, 232
    app development, 233
    generated text, 237
    init() function, 236
    processInput() function, 234
    temperature, 232
    testing, 236
    updateSliders() function, 235

M

Machine learning (ML) model, 20
    accessibility, 3
    adequate model, 20
        architecture, 23
        connectionism field, 23
        cost-effectiveness, 5
        data, 20
            continuous variables, 22
            discrete variable, 22
            exploratory data analysis, 21
            types, 21
        deploying model, 26
        deployment platform, 20
        evaluation phase, 25
        JavaScript, 2
        loss function, 24
        no free lunch theorem, 22
        optimizer, 24
        performance metric, 20, 23
        privacy, 4
        speed, 4
        TensorFlow.js (*see*
            TensorFlow.js)
        training framework, 20, 23
    means model, ml5.js library, 78
Mean squared error (MSE), 64
Modified National Institute of
        Standards and Technology
        (MNIST) digits, 96, 97

N

Node.js, 185
    interactive shell, 272
    MobileNet model, 187
    server creation, 197
        handler function, 199

imageBufferToTensor()
    function, 197
Multer's memoryStorage()
    function, 199
POST route, 199
testing, 200
trainer creation
    environment setup, 188
    functional approach, 193
    getImages() function, 191
    init() function, 195
    installion, 188
    readImage() function, 190
    TensorBoard, 196
    tf.node.tensorBoard()
        callback, 194
    transfer learning, 192
    truncatedModel.predict()
        function, 193
transfer learning, 186

O

Object detection model, 164
    app creation, 173
        CSS code, 175
        detect() function, 178
        drawBoundingBoxes()
            function, 180
        getBoundingBoxes()
            function, 179
        loadObjectDetection()
            function, 177

load packages, 174
prediction object, 179
setupCamera() function, 176
testing, 181
AutoML Vision
    data overview, 166
    definition, 165
    Google Cloud account (*see*
        Google Cloud account)

P, Q

Padding technique, 94
Plotly, 77, 85
PoseNet
    COCO dataset, 128
    game creation, 129
        adjustRules() function, 144
        context methods, 136
        CSS code, 132
        detect() function, 140
        drawKeypoints()
            function, 137
        drawPoint() function, 136
        drawSkeleton() function, 137
        gameplay loop, 141
        getPose() method, 139
        init() function, 135
        initGame() function, 142
        initGameLoop()
            function, 145
        load() method, 138
        loadVideo() function, 134

PoseNet (*cont.*)
MediaDevices.getUser
Media() function, 134
nextPose() function, 142
prediction object, 140
prepareButtons()
function, 148
requestAnimationFrame()
method, 135, 139
resetGame() function, 147
setupCamera() function, 133
testing, 148
UI structure, 129
updateState() function, 144
verifyPose() function, 143
heatmaps, 127
MobileNet-based variant, 128
multiple poses estimator, 126
offset vectors, 127
overview, 125
ResNet variant, 128
single pose estimator, 126

R

Recurrent neural
network (RNN), 203
dataset, 206
recurrent neuron, 204
time series forecasting, 207
app's interface, 207
createButton() function, 218
CSS styles, 210
dataset transformation, 210

defineModel() function, 214
getElementById()
function, 215
index.js script, 209
init() function, 219
initMultiModel()
function, 225
loss value during
training, 230
LSTM layer, 214
multimodel's test case, 227
onBatchEnd loss, 220
onEpochEnd training, 220
predict() function, 216
prepareDataset(), 212, 213
prepareMultiDataset()
function, 222
range-like function, 218
test case, 220, 230, 231
tf.Tensor.arraySync()
method, 223
training's loss value, 227
validation loss, 220
time series forecasting, 204

S

Symbolic tensor, 15

T, U, V, W, X, Y, Z

TensorFlow.js
architecture
tensors, 10

asynchronous code, 279

attributes, 277

backend modes, 7

   CPU, 8

   Node.js, 8

   WebGL, 7

Compatibility with
   TensorFlow, 8

content delivery network, 16

convert to array, 273

external resources, 281

functional model, 276

hyperparameters, 277

immutable, 272

inference engine, 5

installation, 16

layers API, 10, 12

   functional model, 14

   sequential model, 13

mathematical operations, 273

memory management, 273

operations API, 10, 15

pre-trained models, 6

reshaping, 272

sequential model, 276

testing, 278

visualization (tfjs-vis), 274

   distribution values, 275

   model summary, 274

ToxDet, 152

   Google Chrome extension, 154

      callback function, 158

      deployment, 160

      developer mode, 160

      index.html file, 155

      init() function, 158

      manifest.json file, 155

      permissions attribute, 155

      popup.html file, 156

      toxic text and labels, 161

   screenshot, 152

   training dataset, 154

   transfer learning, 153

   universal sentence
      encoder, 152

Toxicity detector model, *see* ToxDet

Made in the USA
Las Vegas, NV
05 December 2020